STYLE
AND THE
MAN

Also by Alan Flusser

Dressing the Man: Mastering
the Art of Permanent Fashion

Clothes and the Man: The Principles of
Fine Men's Dress

Making the Man: The Insider's Guide
to Buying Men's Clothes

STYLE
AND THE
MAN

ALAN FLUSSER

ILLUSTRATIONS BY ANDERS WENNGREN

itbooks

An Imprint of HarperCollins*Publishers*

First It Books edition published 2010.

Designed by Joel Avirom

Typesetting and layouts by Laura Lindgren

The Library of Congress has cataloged the previous edition as follows:
Flusser, Alan.
   Style and the man / Alan Flusser.—1st ed.
       p.   cm.
   ISBN-10: 0-06-270155-X
   1. Men's clothing.   2. Grooming for men.   3. Men's clothing
industry—Guidebooks.   4. Shopping—Guidebooks.

   TT617.F58 G74 1996
   646/.32 21

                                                        96203383

ISBN 978-0-06-197615-5 (2010 edition)

       17 18 19 [WBG/RRD] 10 9 8

———

To Hope and my girls,
Whose laughter and love keep me going

———

A C K N O W L E D G M E N T S

RICHARD LALLY
My new lifetime amigo for his consummate
professionalism and unselfish dedication
to the script at hand

ROBERTO DUTESCO
A photographer of prodigious talent
and a man of uncommon charm

ANDERS WENNGREN
For his museum-quality illustrations

Special mention:
JOSEPH MONTEBELLO, editor extraordinaire
A sartorial angel cloaked in substance and style
whose wisdom shaped our collaboration, so
I could realize my dreams

Sincere thanks to:
Paul Adler, Luciano Barbera, Michel Barnes, Tom Beebe,
G. Bruce Boyer, Bill Brandt, Cameron Buchanan,
John Butcher, John Carnera, Nino Cerruti, Jill Cohen,
Skip Cuddy, Angus Cundley, Martin Flusser, Santo Gallo,
Fred Gates, Ralph Di Gennaro, Robert Gieves,
Robert Gilotte, George Glasgow, Jay Greenfield,
Martin Greenfield, Clifford Grodd, Norman Halsey,
Woody Hochswender, Alexander Kabbaz, Richard Merkin,
Jim Moore, Derrill Osborn, Till Reiter, Andrew Rowley,
Adam Sahmanian, Mark Sahmanian, Ken Spink,
Bobby Taylor, Gaspare Tirone, Stanley Tucker, John Tudor,
Marco Wachter, Ken Williams,
and especially Joel Avirom

CONTENTS

◉—◉

INTRODUCTION

With this, my third book, I hope to take another step toward helping the style-conscious man to help himself. Much of what I have gleaned about sartorial matters is wisdom that was shared with me, so acting as its source for others gives me genuine pleasure. My father's interest in clothes planted the seed when I was very young. Much of what I have learned in traveling the globe to learn the veritics of true style is contained within these pages.

Contrary to the opinons held by many of my colleagues, I believe that dressing well, or in this case, buying clothes wisely, is much less instinctual and arcane than often portrayed. During my thirty years of designing and selling clothes to men, I have found them to be quick studies if given dressing advice that is both demonstrable and rational. And I've yet to meet a man who, in the privacy of the fitting room, will not express an interest in learning how to look better.

Since the most expensive clothes a man will ever buy are those that he rarely wears, this guide trics to offer some insight into how to discern the stylishly classic from the provisionally fashionable. Although this is not a book about dressing as such, the information and illustrations describing how to buy and wear clothes are intended to clarify those issues that must be understood if one is to shop more wisely.

"Who are the well-dressed men of today?" That is the question I am asked more frequently than any other. I usually respond that there are few in the public eye, though I do cite several television newsmen who show some aptitude. This absence of stylish exemplars constitutes a paradox in modern men's fashion. Given this generation's heightened fashion consciousness and the explosive growth of international menswear, how do we explain this dearth of truly well-dressed men?

Many fashion historians consider the 1930s as the epoch of unparalleled elegance in men's clothing. It was certainly a stylish time. Though the world's economies were depressed, men's fashion took its lead from the custom clothes worn by the upper classes, Europe's titled aristocracy, and Hollywood's cinematic royalty. However, the lesson of this era lies not in how extraordinarily well turned-out the privileged few were, but in the fact that the average man's level of dressing sophistication was not far behind. This clearly reflected his access to sound fashion advice and exposure to stylish role models. *Esquire* and *Apparel Arts* magazines, newsreels, films, newspaper and magazine ads, and the window displays and salespeople in fine stores all helped to set dressing standards for a generation.

Despite the commonly held myth that stylish men are born, not made, dressing well is an acquired skill. Becoming proficient in matters of self-attire is much like honing the talents needed to become a great golfer. While playing frequently can improve your game, until you start practicing the correct technique, your potential will always remain unfulfilled. All issues of proportion or design, as they relate to a man's individual style, should have a logical explanation. Unfortunately, much of what passes for expertise today is little more than opinion. Since there are no courses on how to dress well, nor anywhere to go for guidance that is unprejudiced by the prospect of a sale, it is no wonder the modern fashion firmament has produced so few paragons of men's style.

It also hasn't produced the highest caliber of sales

help. As retailers' profits are squeezed by increased over-heads, training and service are the first to suffer. The exceptional salesperson who manifests any real talent is often promoted to management or hired away. And since most trainees have never experienced fine service themselves, it's hard for them to know how to give it. As the price of fine wearables continues to rise, it behooves a man to become more self-sufficient in his pursuit of individual style. As one well-known store's advertising copy reads: "The educated consumer is our best customer." That might better read: "Today's consumer needs to become his own best-educated customer."

STYLE
AND THE
MAN

How to
Buy and Wear...

TAILORED CLOTHING

Since the price of a suit constitutes most men's single largest clothing outlay, unless you are confident of your ability to select the best one, I recommend that you prepare accordingly. Wearing something that is reasonably representative of what you are shopping for provides the salesman with a starting point and the fitter with a tailoring guide. If you are considering a different take on your usual habiliments, this same garment can also provide a basis for comparison.

Should you go to the store intending to make a purchase, you should bring a dress shirt whose fit satisfies you. The dress shirt is a key element in the suit-fitting process; its collar height and sleeve length inform the tailor how you expect those components of the jacket to fit. You should also bring along all the items you normally pack into your suit. If you wear a pocket square or an eyeglass case in your jacket, or keep a wallet in your back trouser pocket, your suit should be fitted to accommodate these items. The time invested in this preparation will minimize the probability that you will have to return to the store for an additional fitting after discovering that your bulging billfold makes your coat's chest gap.

If you are shopping in a large store that offers a variety of suit styles—such as London's Harrods or New York City's Saks Fifth Avenue—and you do not have a relationship with any of its salespeople, spend a few minutes looking for one whose dressing style impresses you. Do not automatically accept the first sales associate to engage you unless you know exactly what you want and need him to act merely as an expediter. If you are looking for a high-fashion designer suit, the traditionally attired salesperson would not be my first choice to explain the nuances distinguishing a Ralph Lauren Black Label suit from the latest Giorgio Armani confection.

Alternatively, if you like to accessorize your moderately priced suits with more expensive, high-class furnishings, you might want to be attended to by someone whose taste demonstrates firsthand experience in such matters. The salesman who dresses as if he is interested in clothes usually regards his profession as something more than just an opportunity to bring home a regular paycheck. He prides himself on his taste and enjoys taking the extra effort to find something special. Ideally, in the course of your dialogue, he should be able to teach you something about how to dress better while assisting you with your decision making.

FIT AND FABRIC

At the turn of the twenty-first century, better men's tailored clothes fell into two general silhouettes, the English/ Milanese custom-tailored look and the contemporary designer look of Giorgio Armani's fuller, languid, drapey swathings. Today, the English/Milanese genre has evolved into a slightly more fitted version of itself, albeit still soft and lightweight on the body, while the designer-inspired suit has morphed into an updated rendition of the Pierre Cardin hourglass suit of the 1970s, sans the rope shoulders and flared legs. The new suit has a younger, trimmer, closer-to-the-body sensibility with lower-rise, plain-front trousers completing the look.

Because both shapes of clothing rely on a more defined line to accomplish their goals, suit fabrics have returned to the harder finished worsteds that used to be associated with the English persuasion of dress. The crepelike, drapey fabrics of the Armani era have basically been retired to make way for these new English and Italian lighter-weight four-harness cloths, their tighter weaves and more substantial construction made to feel soft and pliable courtesy of the technological advances made in dyeing, spinning, and weaving finer-count worsted yarns.

In the case of the newest designer-inspired, body-conscious silhouette, the fabric emphasis is on sleekness, meaning dark dressy worsteds that can do double duty as a business suit by day and an open-collar outfit by night. Because the jacket is generally solid or striped and dark in nature, it can also lose the pants and host a pair of jeans and a tieless dress shirt for duty out of the office. Because of the new suit's sexier yet classic lines, it has sparked young men's interest in tailored clothing, as they can see the garment's potential for fashionable versatility.

In fact, you could say that the two generic suit silhouettes are as much defined by their respective trouser shapes as anything else. Whereas the updated lines of the classic custom-tailor-inspired suit silhouette can accommodate a fuller-fitting pleated or plain-front trouser, the new designer silhouette demands a slimmer-fitting, lower-rise, plain-front trouser.

Unfortunately, the new designer silhouette's weakest style link is that the waist of its jacket buttons is so far above its lower-sitting trouser's waistband that it exposes a patch of dress shirt and belt buckle below. There is nothing like a low-slung trouser with visible belt buckle to draw attention to itself as it cuts the wearer in half while shortening his leg line. Hopefully, as the fashion initiate's tastes mature, he will come to understand the more flattering harmony that needs to be struck between the suit trouser, belt buckle, and suit jacket's waistline.

ASSESSING A SUIT'S LONGEVITY

No other garment in the history of fashion better connotes an image of formal continuity and authority than the man's tailored suit jacket. The permanence of its form relies on a set of design relationships whose formal composition accommodates a surprising variety of improvisations without compromising its aesthetic integrity. Since the Peacock Revolution in the 1960s, fashion design has remolded the suit's envelope into temporal configurations ranging from boxy and short to tight and long, each with its own arrangement of fabric, detail, and trim. Yet, despite the fashion designer's seemingly congenital predisposition for reworking the tailored men's jacket into his own image, as the new century unfolds, the lines of the classically tailored suit jacket have basically survived while continuing to inform the universal standard for civility and continuity in masculine stylishness.

While fabrics and patterns usually attract the eye first, the most important consideration in evaluating any garment is its proportions in relation to the wearer. Most suits are constructed to provide at least several years of wear; however, it's the suit's proportions that will ultimately determine its potential lifetime.

In assessing a jacket's potential life span, four elements of its design should be considered. These are the garment's "bones." When in accordance with the wearer's architecture, they should flatter and enhance his stature. If the coat's architecture fails to harmonize with that of the wearer, the coat's fashion longevity will be significantly reduced.

THE SHOULDERS

As the widest part of the jacket, the shoulders' expression sets the mood for the entire garment. The assertive eighties saw jacket shoulders attain aircraft carrier dimensions, while the introspective nineties returned the shoulders to a less obtrusive, more classic positioning. Most of history's best-dressed men had their jacket shoulders tailored to look natural yet smart. Unless a man is extremely slope-shouldered or self-consciously short and needs the illusion of height, padded shoulders should be avoided.

SHOULDERS CUT TOO WIDE DIMINISH THE HEAD.

In the late 1950s, the square, high-shoulder look became internationally fashionable with the emergence of Rome's "Continental look." Then, in the late sixties, Pierre Cardin's hourglass-shaped suit with its high-roped shoulders reinforced the notion that a strongly defined shoulder line somehow equated to high style. However, even in Italy, the sculpted shoulder's birthplace, the sophisticated Italian sports his hand-tailored shoulders soft, sloped, and less studied.

SHOULDERS CUT TOO NARROW MAKE THE HEAD APPEAR LARGER THAN IT IS.

Close attention also needs to be paid to the jacket shoulders' width. Since they frame the head, if the shoulders are cut too narrow, the head will appear larger than it actually is; if they are cut too wide, the head will appear disproportionately small.

THE JACKET'S SHOULDERS FRAME THE HEAD—A BALANCED PRESENTATION.

FULLNESS OVER THE BLADES
ALLOWS THE JACKET TO
DRAPE COMFORTABLY AND
RELEASES THE ARMS TO
MOVE FREELY.

The shoulders' width should be generous enough to permit the jacket's fabric to fall from the shoulder in a smooth, unbroken line all the way down the sleeve. If the width hugs too narrowly, the man's shoulder muscle will bulge out from under the top of the sleeve head, that point at which the jacket sleeve is attached to the shoulder.

The jacket also needs enough fullness across the front and back to lie flat on a man's chest without pulling open. A man with a strong chest requires a larger sized jacket just to accommodate this prominence. Fullness over the shoulder blades with breaks extending upward on the back from below the armholes allows ample room for free action. This extra fabric also causes the jacket to drape properly. A tight fit over the shoulder blades can make you feel as if you are in a straitjacket.

Jacket shoulders forming sharp, square angles on either side of the head create an artificial formality. The legendary best-dressed set have always been distinguished by an understated naturalness and lack of self-consciousness. The more aggressive the jacket's shoulder line, the more it looks like the wearer is trying to appear more important than he actually feels.

JACKET LENGTH

The correct length of an average man's jacket can vary up to ½ inch without compromising its longevity. Altering its length can play havoc with the hip pockets, moving them out of balance with the whole. Your appropriate jacket length can be established using several methods. Regardless of which is chosen, one principle must be kept in mind: the coat has to be long enough to cover the curvature of a man's buttocks while giving him as long a leg line as possible.

The first approach utilizes the arm as a guide, the other the torso. With the first method, a man uses the knuckle of his thumb to line up the bottom of his jacket. Though generally reliable, this formula has one drawback. A man with a short or average torso but long arms can end up with too long a coat. While its hip pockets may be more accessible, its excess length will swallow up his legs.

METHOD 1: JACKET LENGTH IN RELATION TO THE ARM. RULE OF THUMB: JACKET'S BOTTOM SHOULD LINE UP WITH THUMB KNUCKLE.

Employing the second method, the tailor measures from under the jacket's back collar, where the collar is joined to the coat's body, down to the floor and divides by two.

In the absence of a jacket, a buttoned shirt collar may be substituted as a starting point. This is the procedure taught in all formal tailoring schools. Both guidelines originated with America's introduction of ready-made tailored clothing for men, which needed to establish guidelines upon which to base its standards of fit. However, since either of these can be influenced by dimensions unique to the wearer's

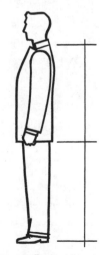

METHOD 2: JACKET LENGTH IN RELATION TO THE TORSO. DIVIDE THE DISTANCE FROM THE COLLAR'S SEAM TO THE FLOOR IN HALF.

physique, a top custom tailor or experienced fitter will trust his learned eye to take in the whole picture before deciding on the jacket's ideal length.

The Waist Button

The waist button is to a suit jacket what the fulcrum is to a seesaw. If it's off center, a delicate balance is lost. When the waist button is fastened, the entire body should be in ideal proportion, with both legs and torso appearing at their maximum length. Since the waist button functions as an axis, raise it and you abbreviate the torso, lower it and the torso elongates but the leg line is shortened.

The correct placement of this critical element occurs $1/2$ inch below the natural waist. To find your natural waist, put your hands around the smallest part of your torso. With the suit jacket's final fitting, most custom tailors will pull on the fastened waist button to confirm that there is enough fullness in the jacket's waist while observing how the coat moves on the body. An incorrectly positioned waist button calls the garment's pedigree into immediate question.

The Gorge

The gorge is that point where the collar and lapel meet. The coat's design determines its height. While there is some flexibility in its placement on the upper chest, raise or lower it too much from its ideal height and you court instant obsolescence. One American designer used to place his label's gorge so high on the collarbone as to make the coat appear to be moving backwards. Conversely, in the late 1980s Giorgio Armani dropped his so low, they are now decorating the backs of their owners' closets. Like the jacket waist button, the gorge's placement needs to help give the wearer height and still look natural on his chest.

Thirty-five years ago, this design element was never an issue. Today if the jacket's gorge is out of sync it is usually because its placement is too low. Done initially to loosen up the coat's starchiness, dropping the gorge too low also loosens up the coat's longevity. Like all elements of classic design, the placement of the gorge should follow geometric logic, not the arbitrariness of fashion.

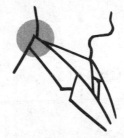

JACKET COLLAR NEEDS
TO BE LOWERED.

JACKET COLLAR NEEDS
TO BE RAISED.

INTO THE FITTING ROOM

Proper fitting can do much for a less costly suit, while a poor fit can scuttle the most expensively hand-tailored creation. If a $3,000 suit's collar is bouncing off your neck as you walk, the suit's value will be severely compromised. The jacket collar that creeps up or stands away from your neck is the fault of the tailor, unless he fit it while you assumed a posture other than your normal one. When standing in front of the tailor's mirror, relax. Do not stand at attention unless that is your natural stance. Standing overly erect can affect the way the tailor fits the jacket collar to your neck.

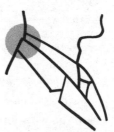

CORRECT RELATIONSHIP: As
½ INCH OF THE SHIRTSLEEVE
SHOULD SHOW BELOW THE JACKET
CUFF, ½ INCH OF THE SHIRT
COLLAR SHOULD APPEAR
ABOVE THE JACKET COLLAR.

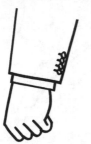

DRESSING THE HAND:
A ½-INCH BAND OF LINEN
SHOULD SHOW BELOW
THE JACKET CUFF.

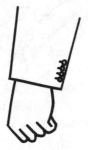

MOST MEN WEAR
THEIR COAT SLEEVES
TOO LONG.

Collar alterations will be even more accurate if you wear a dress shirt, whose collar height can be used by the fitter as a guide. There should be ½ inch of the shirt's collar showing above the jacket; ¾ inch should be exposed when wearing a wing collar with a dinner jacket.

Since there should be the same amount of linen rising above the jacket's collar as that which peeks out from under its sleeve, let's move on to sleeve length. Ninety percent of all men wear their coat sleeves too long and therefore are unable to show that ½ inch of shirt cuff that dresses the hand of any well-attired gentleman. Since most dress shirt sleeves either shrink or are bought too short, they cannot be seen even if the jacket's sleeves have been correctly fitted. Most tailors, in an effort to cover the wrist, finish the coat sleeve where the shirt sleeve is supposed to end. (For an explanation of the dress shirt sleeve's proper fit, see page 34.) The jacket sleeve should extend to where the wrist breaks with the hand. This length should reveal ½ inch of the shirt cuff. The band of linen between sleeve and hand, like that above the jacket collar, is one of the details that define the sophisticated dresser.

VENTS

The ventless jacket gives the hip a cleaner, more slimming line while lending the suit a dressier stature. Though aesthetically pleasing, ventless backs lack function, as they prevent easy access to the trouser pockets in addition to wrinkling more easily from sitting. However, as this back gives a man's torso a leaner, sexier shape, most men ignore its inconvenience.

The center vent, an American predilection, is the least aesthetic venting option, though it offers more utility than having no vent at all. While perfectly designed for spreading the two sides of a rider's jacket across the saddle of a horse, its original intention, the single vent looks awful when a man, having put his hand in his trouser or jacket pocket, pulls it open to reveal his derriere and, if the vent is cut high enough, a fringe of disordered shirt. Savile Row custom tailors avoid the center vent like the plague unless it is imposed upon them by a visitor from the Colonies. The single vent's only saving grace may be that it can be altered to better conceal a prominent hip than either the ready-made ventless or double-vented jacket.

The double vent or side slit offers the best combination of function and form. When you put your hands in your trouser pockets, the side vent's flap stays down, covering the buttocks. If you are seated, the flap moves away, thereby minimizing creasing. Most men shy away from side vents because getting them to fall correctly requires more attention. When fit properly, however, the jacket's two slits trace the outside lines of the body. An illusion of height is also created, because the side vent moves the observer's eye up from the bottom of the jacket. Since double-vented coats are costlier to manufacture and more difficult to fit than other models, you see them less frequently. However, the well-designed side-vented jacket gives its wearer a dash of style that bespeaks its English pedigree and custom-tailored tradition.

VESTS

Most men's suits come two-piece, since adding a third element increases their price. However, the vest has always been favored by those style-conscious men who appreciate the quiet resplendence of a third layer of wool. The businessman in his three-piece suit who removes his jacket in the office can rely on the dressiness of his waistcoat to retain some decorum while enjoying the freedom of shirtsleeved attire. A vest also augments a suit's versatility, as its exclusion from a three-piece ensemble creates a different look.

The properly fitted vest should be long enough for its fifth button from the top to cover the trouser waistband, yet not so long that its points extend below the hip. A well-made vest has its own definite waistline, which is where the trouser waistband should hit. Men who prefer low-rise trousers that rest on the hips should avoid vests. Belts and vests should also choose other dance partners, since belts not only add further bulk to the already layered waistline, but tend to poke out from under the vest. When the suit's trousers are supported by braces, with their pleats spilling out from under the waistcoat, the single-breasted ensemble achieves a tailored swank afforded only by the addition of this third layer.

A waistcoat should not have a skintight fit. It should be cut full enough to allow its wearer to sit comfortably with its back belt done up to keep it from riding up the trouser waistline. The top of the vest should be high enough to peek out above the waist-buttoned coat. A classic suit vest has four welt pockets, with a six-button front designed to leave the bottom button undone. Better-designed vests have their fronts slightly curved to conform to the single-breasted jacket's rounded fronts. A waistcoat's back should be longer than its front. This length is needed to cover the trouser waistband should a man choose to bend forward. The vest's back lining usually matches the jacket's sleeve lining. Vests without adjustable rear belts or whose fronts and backs are of equal length are usually poorly designed and cheaply made.

Right down to its unbuttoned, cutaway bottom, the man's tailored vest is a legacy of upper-class fashion. Even the way it is worn is a tribute to royal style. Having unbuttoned his waistcoat to relieve the pressure on his royal ampleness, Edward VII neglected to do up the bottom vest button at dinner's end. Instead of a sartorial faux pas, an eccentric fashion ensued which survives to this day.

TROUSERS

As it was always intended to, the cut of a suit trouser takes its cue from the shape of the jacket above. Today the trouser falls into two basic fashion stances: the fuller cut, waist-sitting, pleated or plain-front model for the classically shaped jacket and the slimmer cut, lower-rise, plain-front variety for the new fashion-forward designer suit.

The new contemporary suit silhouette features smaller-width shoulders, narrower sleeves, and torso-hugging lines, which in turn demand a trouser whose cut basically harks back to the last time menswear tried converting men away from their baggier business suits and into sexier, more body-conscious vessels—the 1970s, when the new Cardin hourglass-shaped suit became the rage of the fashion-buying universe.

This time around, instead of flaring at the bottom, suit pants are pretty narrow, with not much room in the seat or thigh. Some wristwatch-over-shirt-cuff-wearing Europeans sport theirs on the short side, just above the shoe, trimmed with a wider cuff of 1 inch or more. The new fashion-forward suit trouser comes with belt loops, plain front, and a slightly

THE TROUSER CREASE
SHOULD INTERSECT
THE MIDDLE OF THE
KNEE AND BISECT THE
MIDDLE OF THE SHOE.

lower rise to sit just above the hips. The cut flatters men with a smaller chest and hips with a 36-inch waist or less. Mature male bread-lovers probably need not apply.

As for the classically cut suit jacket, the trouser preference is still for pleats; however, plain fronts are making inroads. The current pleated model that now accompanies most fine tailored suits has forged its own fashion route to where it stands today. During World War II the U.S. government required manufacturers to conserve fabric, retaining their popularity throughout the gray-flannel, Ivy League era.

However by the 1990s, most men's trousers had returned to the natural waist, recovering from the hip-hugging jeans mentality of the 1960s and the tight, plain-front Continental-inspired pant of the 1970s, with longer rises, deeper pleats, fuller-cut thighs tapering down to the ankles, and often suspenders—exactly the way the great tailors originally designed them: to give comfort and follow the natural lines of the body. Today, the latest pleated suit trouser has likewise been tapered down with slightly narrower legs and shallower pleats for a trimmer but comfortable fit.

In defense of pleated trousers, they tend to project a dressier mien than plain fronts. Their fuller fronts provide greater comfort than plain fronts; hips widen when the wearer is seated and pleats can facilitate this shift with less wear to the trouser. Objects placed in a front pocket are better concealed within a pleated trouser than a pleatless one.

The classically designed pleated trouser has two pleats on either side of its fly—a deep one near the fly and a shallower one near the pocket to help keep the main pleat closed. This arrangement maintains the working relationship between the two pleats. The sometime fashion for multiple pleats or some other gimmick of fancified fullness has no place in the well-dressed man's wardrobe.

While having your trousers fitted, make sure the pleats are not opening. Look down to see if each leg's front crease intersects the middle of each kneecap and finishes in the middle of each shoe. If it is off at all, the crease should err toward the inside of the trouser. A crease that falls outside the knee creates the illusion of breadth, something most men prefer to avoid.

The trouser bottom should rest with a slight break on the top of the shoe. It should be long enough to cover the hose when a man is in stride. Its width should cover about two-thirds of the shoe's length. Cuffs give the trouser bottom weight, helping to define the pleat's crease while maintaining the trouser's contact with the shoe. Like any detail of classic tailoring, cuff width should be neither so narrow nor so wide that it calls attention to itself. To provide the proper balance, the cuffs should be 1⅝ inches for a person under five feet ten, 1¾ inches if he is taller. Cuffs of 1¼ inches or 2 inches reflect the erraticness and impermanence of their master: fashion.

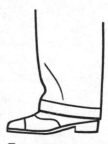

THE WEIGHT OF THE CUFF HELPS KEEP THE TROUSER ON THE SHOE. THE TROUSER BOTTOM SHOULD COVER TWO-THIRDS OF THE WEARER'S SHOE AND BE LONG ENOUGH TO REMAIN IN CONTACT WITH THE SHOE WHEN WALKING.

QUALITY

With the transformation of the men's suit business into a world of designer fashion and the almost complete mechanization of its manufacturing process, determining the contemporary suit's quality and intrinsic value is the most elusive challenge facing today's shopper. Like women's ready-to-wear, the majority of men's tailored clothing today is sold on its name recognition, fit, and aura of fashionability. The era when men's suits were expected to carry a man from one decade to another and were purveyed based on the relative merits of their quality and hand tailoring is as dated as sized hosiery, exact-sleeved dress shirts, and the three-piece suit.

Except for a handful of factories left in the world that continue to tailor suits primarily by hand, most clothing manufacturers have either incorporated the latest technology into their production process or closed shop. The cost of skilled labor and the time required to create a garment in the old-world manner have limited this wearable's market to those retailers and consumers who appreciate the quality and work behind the hand-stitched garment's higher price. In his hallowed fitting rooms, the specialty retailer must be able to explain the nuances of this handcrafted creation from its silk thread and handmade buttonholes to the superiority of its worsted fabric.

Beginning in the 1920s, before machines started replacing tailors, suits were graded from 1 to 6 in a system that specified the number of hand operations used to create the final product. For instance, a number 1, the lowest grade of suit, was almost entirely machine-made. A number 2 coat could use some handwork to finish the cuffs, collar, and buttons. A number 3 had to have these three components finished by hand. A number 6, the highest grade on the scale, was made almost entirely by hand. Of course, some manufacturers would misrepresent these numbers in an attempt to sell their product at a higher quality rating than it deserved, but at least the system gave the retailer and consumer some sort of uniform standard.

As technical improvements in machine-made clothes

blurred the advantages of more costly hand crafting, tailored clothes have become creations of refined engineering and industrialized production. With the tailor's shears and hand-sewn stitches being replaced by computers, laser knives, conveyor belts, fusing, and high speed pressing machinery, the modern men's suit has become a marvel of tailoring science and technological genius. And as with any automated creation, the measure of its quality is time, in this case minutes.

The opening-price suit that sells for $395 takes approximately 80 minutes of uninterrupted labor, while the higher-profile designer garment retailing for $1,495 requires approximately 150 minutes of continuous construction. In other words, little more than an hour of actual labor and quality control separate the least costly from the more expensive designer-name suit. While the higher-priced suit's shell fabric, linings, facings, and fusibles are more costly and produce a softer, more flexible garment, they do not account for the entire difference in retail price. A good part of the disparity represents the expenses involved in operating a high-profile designer fashion business: publicity, advertising, fashion shows, and the overhead of a design studio.

Today, most men's suits are constructed in the same manner as a dress shirt's collars and cuffs, whose outside layers are top-fused for permanent smoothness. First developed during the 1950s, the process of bonding or gluing a layer to an outside shell fabric has evolved to a level where it can nearly simulate the softness and flexibility of the hand-sewn canvas used in tailored men's clothes. Formerly, this layer of reinforcement placed between the coat's outer cloth and inner lining consisted of one or more ply of horsehair and regular canvas secured by numerous hand stitches. When suspended by the elasticity of its handmade silk stitches, its free-floating dynamic gave the jacket's front a lasting shapeliness and drape while lending pliancy and spring to the roll of its lapel. The scientific advances seen in the development and performance of the new fusibles have enabled mechanized tailoring to supplant the more traditional artisan methods. With the consumer requesting lighter, softer tailored clothing, these fusibles allow a coat to mold to the wearer, though they sacrifice fit and longevity in the process.

So, how does a man cut through all this industry mumbo jumbo to determine his prospective suit's level of quality? The answer is complex and difficult to translate into the written word, since these automated garments lack the visible handwork of top quality tailoring to act as benchmarks. The cost efficiency of the new technology encourages manufacturers to incorporate many of the details associated with more expensive tailored clothes into less costly products, rendering the ranking of quality even less clear. Crotch pieces and lined knees are no longer the exclusive province of the most expensively tailored suit trousers, while underarm sweat shields and machine stitching that appears handsewn grace jackets with less than lofty pedigrees.

I will break down the subject into price brackets that represent various generic methods of manufacture so our investigation will have some boundaries and focus. Please remember that this is a discussion about the quality of the product's construction, not the beauty of its design. As you will learn later, a wearable's longevity is predicated more on its design than its quality. A well-designed $350 suit can provide more years of wear than an expensive hand-tailored worsted cashmere suit whose shoulders look as though the hanger is still holding them up.

The best quality ready-made suits are constructed like those that are made by a fine custom tailor, except the workplace has been organized into a miniature factory. This means each garment is individually hand-cut with scissors; the chest, lapels, collar, armholes, buttonholes, lining, pockets, and sleeves have all been sewn by hand; and everything is hand-pressed. At this level of quality, the construction or padding of the jacket's lapels and collar is stitched totally by hand. There could be two thousand stitches or more in a single-breasted jacket's lapel; these will hold the garment's shape intact through all weathers, fair or foul. For this rarefied ready-made suit, one must expect to pay at least $3,000.

The next ministep below this level of quality can boast the same level of workmanship, but the time-consuming lapel hand-basting is done by a special machine. Those parts of the coat that need flexibility and movement continue to be sewn by hand—armholes, shoulders, collar. At a minimum, you should be able to look at the inside of the jacket and confirm that the felling of its linings in these areas is hand-done. Next, you should take the coat's bottom front, three inches from its bottom and two inches from its edge. Rub it between your finger and thumb to feel if there are three distinct layers. You should be able to detect a floating canvas piece sandwiched between the coat's outer shell and inner lining. This confirms the coat has a canvas front rather than a fused one. It is the work of a tailor and the garment's shape will remain intact as long as it is well cared for. Selling for between $1,500 and $2,500, canvas-front retails will endure the ravages of extended wear.

Moving down to the next level of quality, you find the semitraditional or semi-canvas-front coat whose bottom front is fused but not its lapels, collar, and chest. Its canvas inner lining floats, held in place by hand stitches so it moves more naturally with the coat. The beauty of this hybrid is that its lapels roll and stay on the coat's chest more naturally than fused lapels will. The canvas inner lining gives the lapels more spring so that their edges remain in contact with the jacket's chest. One can always tell a fused lapel because its edges tend to curl away from the jacket. The semitraditional make has its shoulders, armholes, and collar handstitched so that the presentation around the man's face and upper torso appears supple and rich. The cost for such a suit usually falls between $850 and $1,200.

The majority of today's tailored clothing is sewn completely by machine and constructed through fusing. One version is made "open" or in what we call the American system. Parts such as the sleeves and collars are assembled separately first, then put together. In the "two-shell" or German system, the entire inside lining shell is assembled separately from the outside fabric shell. Then the one is sewn inside the other. The two-shell calls for less labor and prides itself on its consistency. While requiring additional manufacturing steps, the American system utilizes more basting stitches, elements of make that in the end come out of the coat but help build in its enduring shape. The price of this type of garment can range wildly, from $395 up to $1,495 depending on whose label is inside.

The only thing one needs to consider when making a choice between the two least expensive methods of tailoring is alterability. Most men would never even consider this factor, but they must. Since the two-shell garment has only a ⅜-inch outlet left in its seams, the man who gains ten pounds or more will find it impossible to have the coat let out. Imagine spending $800 on a suit only to find out it cannot be altered to accommodate a change in your physique. I would lean toward the garment made in the traditional open way because its shape comes from building in curves while the engineered coat's shape, due to its flat, straight-lined approach to make, will lose its shapeliness faster.

In conclusion, I would like to remind you that the

aforementioned has been written as a general guide. Within each of these categories, you will encounter garments that resist easy classification. I hope the information passed on here will enable you to ask the correct questions when trying to get a grip on this difficult subject.

SHOPPING AND THE BODY TYPE

Whether short or tall, portly or slim, a man needs to shop for his clothing with his individual physique in mind. Since most people aspire to look like some idealized version of themselves, selecting clothes based on a particular body type is as old as fashion itself. Whereas I believe that familiarity with the geometric principles that downplay girth or emphasize height or breadth is helpful, such information should be viewed as a guide rather than dogma.

I have seen the most well-dressed men wear clothes in stark contradiction to the accepted dictates of fashionable physiognomy. I can recall one portly, older gentleman looking so debonair in his large, plaid, hefty tweed sports suit simply because it was cut to perfection. I am told that no other group of men would parade down Savile Row in the thirties with more panache than the contingent of Brazilian diplomats, most of whom were under five feet seven and all of whom wore their soft-shouldered, double-breasted suits with cuffed trousers. Proportion in dress is the foundation of all classic dressing. The truly stylish man knows enough about the rules to know how and when to break them.

To assist some of the basic body types in choosing their tailored clothing, I would like to make the following suggestions:

Short, Slim Men

Clothes should elongate and add shaped fullness.

Jackets
1.   Shoulder can be higher and slightly broader.
2.   Torso should broaden the chest and shoulders and have slight waist suppression.
3.   Jacket length should be as short as possible, however, covering the buttocks without cutting the wearer in two.
4.   Single-breasted, two-button jackets are always appropriate.
5.   Single-breasted, three-button coats promote a longer line.
6.   Double-breasted coats should have a long roll and button below the natural waist.
7.   Lapel notches should be in the chest's upper range. Peaked lapels offer more height.
8.   Side vents or no vents.
9.   Flap pockets add more width to the hip and balance better with the wider shoulder, but they are not as elongating as the simple besom pocket.
10. Long sleeves make a short man look overcoated.
11. Fabrics such as mill-finished worsteds and flannels; with patterning that emphasizes verticality such as herringbones, medium-spaced chalk or pinstripes, and windowpanes longer in the woof (vertical) than the weft (horizontal).

Trousers
1.   A matching trouser lengthens more than a contrasting one.
2.   Should be worn high on the natural waist to promote a longer leg line and to smooth the transition of jacket to trouser.

3. Trouser should break on shoe to extend the view from top to bottom.
4. Cuffs (1⅝ inches) help to smooth the transition of the fuller trouser with the larger scale shoe.

Accessories
1. Striped dress shirts with noncontrasting collars and cuffs.
2. Spread collars, tab collars, long pointed pinned collars.
3. Suspenders emphasize verticality.
4. Striped, solid, understated neckwear knotted in four-in-hand style.
5. Necktie length should finish no lower than the belt line—for longer neckties, retie them so front blade is shorter and then tuck longer back blade through keeper into trouser.
6. Handkerchief folded with points leaning outward.
7. Welted-soled shoes add height and balance with the breadth of the shoulder.

SHORT, HEAVY MEN

Clothes should also elongate but work to deemphasize breadth.

Jackets
1. Straighter-cut coat.
2. Two-button single-breasted better than three-button or double-breasted.
3. Flap pockets better balance wider shoulders.
4. Side vents over no vents.
5. Sleeves need to taper down to cuff, cannot be too wide at hand.
6. Fabrics should be dark and smooth, such as fine worsteds.

7. Dark solids, medium-width stripings, and herringbones deemphasize bulk.

Trousers

1. Reverse pleat on trouser keeps front flat while breaking the expanse of its width.
2. As long a rise as comfortable, fit on natural waist not below protruding stomach.
3. Cuffs assist the transition of the full-cut trouser to the larger-scaled shoe.

Accessories

1. Long straight point collars.
2. Solid ties; patterened ties; ties with stripes or prints with movement.
3. Welt-sole shoes for a more substantial platform; no lightweight, dainty footwear.

TALL MEN

The taller the tree, the broader its branches, so the tall man needs fuller cut clothes for balance and style. The selections should deemphasize length by breaking up the vertical lines.

Jackets

1. Sloping shoulders of generous width.
2. Coat should be cut on the longer side.
3. Double-breasted model that buttons on waist, not below it, such as the six-on-two formation.
4. Two- or three-button single-breasted.
5. Broader lapels, finishing in lower area of upper chest.
6. Flap pockets and the additional ticket pocket help fragment verticality.
7. The fabrics can be heavier in look, such as flannels and

cheviots, and of larger scale in pattern, such as broad stripes, houndstooth checks, glen plaids, or squared-off windowpanes.

Trousers
1. Long rise, full cut with deep pleats.
2. Legs with gentle taper.
3. Cuffs (1¾ inches) with definite break on shoe.

Accessories
1. Full-cut shirts must show ½ inch of shirt cuff.
2. White contrast collars and cuffs break up length.
3. Amply proportioned spread collars.
4. Broadly spaced, fine-lined stripes, tattersall checks, windowpanes, and horizontal stripes.
5. Belts break up length.
6. Welt-soled shoes for more substantial foundation.

ATHLETIC BUILD

For the man of average height whose chest size is at least eight inches more than his waist size, the principle is to reproportion the oversized shoulder with the smaller bottom.

Jackets
1. Shoulders should be as unpadded and natural-looking as possible.
2. Jackets need length to balance the strong shoulder without shortening the leg line.
3. Minimal waist suppression.
4. Two-button single-breasted over double-breasted—avoid three-button single-breasted.
5. Lapels should be full with slight belly.

6. Flaps on pockets.
7. Side vents or no vents.
8. Fabrics should deemphasize bulk: solid worsteds, herringbones, vertical windowpanes, subtle stripes with no less than ¾ inch spacing.

Trousers

1. To fill out the jacket, trousers must be worn as high on waist as comfortable.
2. Full cut through hip and thigh tapering down to 1¾-inch cuff.
3. Trouser leg should have definite break on shoe.

Accessories

Assuming a broad face and thick neck:

1. Vertical shirt collars such as tab or long points.
2. Solid, striped, or patterned neckwear.
3. Shirts with strong stripes.
4. Larger-scale shoes to balance upper heft.

THE DRESS SHIRT

THE DRESS SHIRT COLLAR

When purchasing a dress shirt—that is, one intended to be worn with a necktie—consider its collar first. Regardless of whether the shirt appears to go perfectly with your new suit, or is meticulously crafted with vast numbers of stitches to the inch, or even woven in the Caribbean's most lustrous sea island cotton, if its high-banded collar looks as if it might swallow up your neck or its diminutive collar makes your already prominent chin appear more so, move on. You need to focus on that portion of the dress shirt responsible for exhibiting to best advantage the body part that should receive the most attention—your face.

The triangle formed by the V opening of a buttoned tailored jacket and extending up to the area just below a person's chin is the cynosure of a man's costume. There are several dynamics working simultaneously to direct a viewer's focus toward this sector. First, it is situated directly under the face, the wearer's most expressive body part. Second, the area is usually accentuated by contrasts between the darker jacket and lighter shirt, the jacket and tie, and the tie and dress shirt. This triangular sector offers more visible layers of textural activity than any other part of a man's outfit, and the point at which all these elements converge is directly under one's chin, where the inverted V of the dress shirt collar comes to a point.

Think of your face as a portrait and your shirt collar as its frame. The collar's height on your neck as well as the length and spread of its points should complement the shape and size of your face. Within the infinite permutations of angle, scale, and mass, no single article of apparel better enhances a man's countenance than the well-designed dress shirt collar. Since a person's bone structure is fixed, although it will be affected by a weight gain or loss, the choice of collar should be guided by the individual's particular physical requirements rather than the vicissitudes of fashion. Unlike other less visible accoutrements such as hosiery or shirt cuffs, this focal point constitutes one of a man's most revealing gestures of personal style. All sophisticated dressers have arrived at one or more collar styles

THE CYNOSURE OF
THE TAILORED MAN'S
PRESENTATION.

that best highlight their unique features while managing to add a bit of dash along the way.

Choosing the appropriate shirt collar requires experimentation and common sense. A smallish man with delicate features would be lost in a high-set collar with points longer than 3 inches. Conversely, a heavyset or big-boned man would loom even larger sporting a small collar. Shirt collars should counterbalance the facial structure by either softening its strong lines or strengthening its soft ones. Long straight point collars—those 3 inches or more—will extend and narrow a wide face just as the broad-spaced points of spread collars will offset the line of a long or narrow one.

Tab collars or other pinned collars have the necessary height to shorten long necks. Strong-chinned men require fuller proportioned collars, just as large tabletops clamor for ample pedestals to achieve aesthetic balance. Though, admittedly, button-downs can look casually stylish, they are too often favored by exactly the kind of men who should avoid them—the double chinned set. Softer-chinned men need slightly higher and firmer collars to compensate for the lack of a strong line under their face.

Throughout the eighties and up through the mid-nineties, most dress shirts—no matter how expensive—generally had collars that were too small for the average wearer's face. In an effort to convey a more casual and less structured formality, men's fashion has explored many approaches to neutralizing the collar's conventional starched and ordered format. Consequently, collars have been lowered, shortened, and softened to such degrees that the original precepts for their correct proportioning have been either distorted or lost completely. Button-downs have little or no roll, straight point collars are so short even the smallest tie knot prevents their points from touching the shirt's chest, while spread collars are so low on the neck they have been sapped of all

Straight point collars offset facial rotundity.

Spread collars best present the long or narrow face.

their strength and flair. Except for those produced by a few high-end American, English, and Italian shirtmakers, most dress shirts give the impression they are apologizing for their collars. The explosive growth of the made-to-measure dress shirt business owes much of its prosperity to the scarcity of flatteringly scaled collars on ready-made dress shirts.

Fortunately, men's tailored clothing is segmenting into two distinct mind-sets—dress-up and dress-down. On the dressy side, men who require the services of a jacket and tie are beginning to return to those dress shirts that originally made this uniform so compelling by enabling it to dramatize a man's features. Luckily, today's fashions offer more dress shirts with properly scaled collars than in the last few decades.

As Oscar Schoeffler, longtime fashion editor of *Esquire*, once warned, "Never underestimate the power of what you wear. After all, there is just a small bit of you sticking out at the collar and cuff. The rest of what the world sees is what you drape on your frame." Therefore, the most important factor to weigh when buying a dress shirt isn't its color, fit, or price. It is the collar and its smartness for the wearer's face.

Fit

Other than the Italians, who are almost fetishistically meticulous about the fit of their dress shirts, most men wear theirs too short in the sleeve, too small in the collar, and too full around the wrist. The explanation for this is relatively straightforward: successive washings shrink collar size and sleeve length, while most shirting manufacturers allow enough breadth in a man's cuff to accommodate a large wrist girded by a Rolex-type watch.

The best dress shirt is useless if its collar does not fit comfortably. With the top button closed, you should be able to slide two fingers between the neck and the collar of a new dress shirt. Most better dress shirt makers add an extra 1/2 inch to the stated collar size to allow for shrinkage within the first several washings. I would never wear a new dress shirt unless it fit big in the collar prior to its first washing. If it fits perfectly around the neck in the store or when first tried on at home, return it or risk being strangled by a smaller collar before too very long.

The back of the shirt collar should be high enough to show ½ inch above the rear portion of the jacket's collar (see page 13). Its points should be able to touch the shirt's body and rest smoothly on its front. When a tie is fitted up into the collar, its points should be long enough to remain in contact with the shirt's body, regardless of how sharply the wearer turns his head. No part of the collar's band should be able to be seen peeking over the tie's knot. Semispread to cutaway collars should have no tie space above the tie's knot. In other words, both sides of the collar's inverted V should meet or touch each other while the edges of their points should be covered by the jacket's neck.

WELL-DESIGNED SPREAD COLLARS SHOULD HAVE NO TIE SPACE.

THE EDGES OF A SPREAD-COLLAR DRESS SHIRT SHOULD BE COVERED BY THE JACKET FRONT.

DRESSING THE HAND

The band of linen between coat sleeve and hand is another one of those stylistic gestures associated with the better-dressed man. It has been so ever since the first aristocrat wore his lace ruffles spilling out from beneath his jacket cuffs. Some fashion historians mark the decline in modern men's style from the point at which ready-made buttoned cuffs replaced cuff-linked ones and men found their wrists

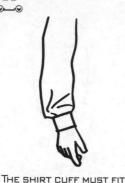

THE SHIRT CUFF MUST FIT
SNUGLY, SO THAT THE
ADDITIONAL SLEEVE
LENGTH WILL NOT FALL
OVER THE HAND.

swathed in excess fabric which either fell down their wrists or pulled up too short.

Whether you choose a button cuff or a French cuff, the shirt cuff should fit snugly around the wrist so that the additional length required to keep it from moving as the arm stretches does not fall down over the hand. If you can slide your hand through the cuff opening without first unfastening it, the shirt's cuff is too large. If the sleeve is long enough and the cuff fits correctly, you should be able to move your arm in any direction without influencing how the cuff rests around your wrist. The shirt cuff and hand should be able to move as a unit.

THE BODY

THE SLEEVE MUST HAVE
ENOUGH LENGTH FOR THE
ARM TO BEND WITHOUT
PULLING ON THE CUFF.

During the 1960s peacock era, when dress shirts had the fit of a second skin and were worn to flaunt the chest and arm muscles, the wearer had to pay particular attention to gaping shirt-fronts if he inhaled too deeply or sat down. Today, with comfort driving the fit of men's clothes, issues such as these are no longer of much concern.

The shirt should certainly be full enough to allow its wearer to sit without concern. Normal shrinkage or a slight weight gain should not render it uncomfortable across the chest or waist. Since shirts with blousier fits tend to have lower armholes, one should pay attention that the jacket's armhole does not pull up the shirtsleeve, making it too short to rest on the top of the hand. A shirt's armhole should fit comfortably up into the armpit for easier movement and consistent length. The shirt's overall length should be such that you can raise your arms without pulling the garment out of the trouser top.

IN CONSIDERATION OF QUALITY

The most expensive component of any dress shirt is its fabric. As the layer in closest contact with the wearer's skin, the most comfortable and luxurious fiber to wear is unquestionably 100 percent cotton. Anyone doubting this need only examine the fiber content of almost all men's undergarments.

Better dress shirts are made in two-ply cotton or twofold yarns, less expensive ones in single-ply. Cotton-poly blends are never two-ply, therefore these fabrics tend to be found only in cheaper shirts. In a true two-ply fabric, the yarns used in the vertical warp and horizontal weft are made from two fibers long enough to twist around each other to produce the incremental strength, silkiness, and luster associated with the two-fold luxury fabric. The finer the yarn, the higher its threads-per-inch count. Two-ply fabrics start at 80/2 (the 2 representing two-ply) and progress to as fine as 220/2 (which feels more like silk than cotton and is so expensive it is used only in custom-made shirts). Two-ply fabrics are typically found in the upper climes of the custom shirt trade. Since two-ply dress shirts are costlier, most manufacturers will include this designation on the label. If it is not so designated, it usually means the shirt is of a single-ply fabric and its cost should reflect this.

Most two-ply cotton shirts begin retailing at $95 for those privately labeled in large department stores and go to well over $300 for those more highly crafted with finer-count two-ply fabrics. This is not to suggest that single-ply dress shirts are necessarily inferior to or automatically less desirable than two-ply versions. Since we know how a poorly designed collar can scuttle the most expensive dress shirt, the two-ply designation reflects a garment's intrinsic quality and not its relative value.

The better dress shirt is one of the few products whose craft has been relatively uncompromised by modern manufacturing technology. Due to the many pieces that must be put together and the exacting sewing procedures required, there is no substitute for the skilled, highly trained labor needed to produce a fine dress shirt. As it is not covered over by linings and such, a dress shirt's construction, with the exception of collar and cuff, can be more easily evaluated than that of tailored clothing or neckties. All of its stitching, seams, and finishing are plainly exposed to the inquiring eye, especially if one knows what to look for and why.

There can be some details of workmanship that, should even one be found present, signal your investigation is at an end and the shirt's dearer price has been confirmed. Most of these benchmarks are holdovers from a less mechanized age when the standards for deluxe quality were set by bespoke shirtmakers. No manufacturer would willingly invest in the labor required to make such a shirt without ensuring the fabric was of a quality that justified the product's retail price. He would be hard-pressed to recoup the cost of such craftsmanship if it was wasted on a shirt composed of inferior cloth.

The handmade buttonhole is a detail rarely found in shirts made outside of France or Italy. If you have a shirt with handmade buttonholes it represents a piece of workmanship that literally comes from the old country. Now, some custom shirtmakers will argue in favor of a fine machine-made buttonhole over a handmade one, but handmade buttonholes are a mark of top-drawer threads. Ironically, they can be identified only by their imperfect stitches and the difference in appearance between their underside and visible portion.

When dress shirts were worn closely fitted to the torso, their side seams were much in evidence and their width and finishing were considered two of the most important criteria for judging their shirtmaking craft. I can recall visiting Italy during the sixties and observing the Romans wrapped in their skintight, darted blue voile shirts with side seams that seemed to disappear into minute lines that traced the body. These side seams were of a single-needle construction. If the shirt you are considering has this feature, you are no doubt holding a garment that will command a better price.

Single-needle side seams are sewn twice, once up and once down the shirt's seam, using only one needle and leaving just a single row of stitches visible on the outside. This is time-consuming and requires greater skill on the part of the operator than other seams. Most shirts' side seams are sewn on a double-needle machine, which is much faster and produces two rows of visible stitching. Unfortunately, the double-needle side seam can, depending on the quality of its execution, pucker over time due to the thread and fabric's different reactions to washing. However, since most modern shoppers are not that informed, the single-needle side seam is rarely found on ready-made shirts, and is almost exclusively reserved for the world of custom shirtmaking.

SINGLE-NEEDLE
SIDE SEAM.

DOUBLE-NEEDLE
SIDE SEAM.

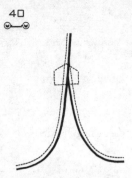

Symbol of old-world workmanship: Reinforcing gusset strengthens and conceals the point at which the shirt's front, back, and side seams join.

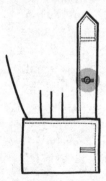

All fine dress shirts should have a buttoning sleeve placket. Evidence of meticulous crafting is the presence of a horizontal buttonhole.

Another telltale sign of an expensively made dress shirt can be found in the bottom tail's design and finishing. Charvet, the famed French *chemisier*, designs its shirts with a square bottom and side slits or vents, which they feel produce less bulk under the trouser. They also believe their deeper sides keep the shirt better anchored. Turnbull and Asser, the Jermyn Street shirtmaker, prefers the rounded bottom but reinforces its side seam at the bottom with a small triangular gusset. Either of these designs demands greater labor and expertise than the typical hemmed bottom. Prior to World War II, the gusset was a common feature on better shirts, but production costs forced many manufacturers to abandon this old-fashioned finishing technique.

The next nuance of detail that signals a dress shirt's loftier pedigree is the direction of its sleeve placket's buttonhole. All better shirts come with a small placket button and buttonhole to close the opening running up the inside sleeve from its cuff. However, a horizontally sewn buttonhole is evidence of meticulous crafting, since the button must be lined up perfectly with the buttonhole, unlike a vertical placement which allows a greater margin for error. Since this detail is easily detectable, it can make any examination a short one.

The last sure giveaway of rarefied
shirtmaking can be detected only in a
shirt made of a striped fabric. Should the
stripe of its sleeve line up exactly with the
horizontal line of the yoke's stripe when
they meet at the shoulder seams, you are
in the presence of shirtmaking art. Generally, this kind of work is reserved for
the custom-made dress shirt, but should
you find it in one ready-made, be prepared to pay at least $300.

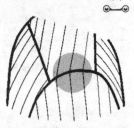

A MATCHING PATTERNED
YOKE TO SLEEVE
IS FOUND ONLY IN A
VERY EXPENSIVE
DRESS SHIRT.

The next passel of workmanship details should be
present on all deluxe-priced ($125 and up) dress shirts,
whether they are representing themselves as better ready-to-
wear, made-to-measure, or even custom-made. While it is
more difficult for the beginner to identify these details, once
learned, less well-made dress shirts become much easier
to spot.

The stitching on a shirt's collar and cuffs should be so
fine as to be nearly invisible. If you can clearly see each individual stitch sitting on top of the fabric, its manufacture is
less costly. All better dress shirt collars have removable
stays. The shape or pattern on either side of a shirt's collar
parts or cuffs should match exactly. Pockets should be lined
up so that they virtually vanish from sight. Buttonholes
should be finished so that it is difficult to see their individual
stitches. Buttons should be cross-stitched for extra strength,
an operation that cannot be performed by machine.

Real pearl buttons are to fine shirts what authentic
horn buttons are to high-quality jackets. If a sewing machine needle hits a plastic button, the button shatters;
should that same needle strike a pearl button, the needle
shatters. Authentic mother-of-pearl buttons, especially
thicker ones, are incredibly sensual to the hand and eye, as

well as costing ten times the price of the typical plastic button.

DRESS SHIRT AESTHETICS

While the dress shirt can function as a backdrop for necktie, braces, jacket, and pocket square, there are two approaches to dress shirt demeanor. The first and by far the more popularly practiced method employs the dress shirt as a neutral foundation. As such, the elements are either harmonized upon it or one is emphasized over the others, such as the patterned tie against a solid shirt. In this presentation, the shirt acts purely in a supporting role.

The alternative approach casts the dress shirt as leading man at center stage. This style emanated from England and is reasonably easy to execute if the principles governing its execution are well understood. In socially conscious London, an upper-class man would signal his membership in a particular club, regiment, or school through his choice of tie. Since these neckties' designs were fairly standard and limited in number (there being, after all, only so many organizations the wearer could claim as his own), he tended to punctuate his somber and predictable business ensembles with more strongly patterned dress shirts, the very reason London's Jermyn Street became so renowned for gentlemen's dress shirts. In this approach, the tie, shirt, and pocket square act as subordinate players to the shirt. A well-endowed collar was essential to convey the shirt's leading role and the wearer's loftier station, which is why English-bred dress shirts tend to have more prominent collars than their European or American counterparts.

As either of these approaches can project considerable sophistication, one last issue remains in guiding a man toward an informed dress shirt purchase. This concerns the stylistic consistency of the shirt's parts. For example, regardless of how beautiful its fabric or fit, a double-breasted jacket with a center vent remains a half-breed, a mixed metaphor, a sartorial mutt. A garment's detailing must be in character with its fabric, or else, like a pinstriped suit with patch pockets or flap pockets on a tuxedo, the wearable's integrity and classiness are compromised.

Here are some general guidelines specific to the styling of men's dress shirts:

The smoother and more lustrous the fabric, the dressier the shirt. On the scale of relative formality, blue broadcloth ranks above blue end-on-end broadcloth, which, in turn, ranks above blue pinpoint oxford, which is finer and dressier than regular blue oxford. But royal or queen's oxford, which is made of a two-ply yarn that gives the oxford weave greater sheen and a finer texture, is comparable to end-on-end broadcloth in its formality. The more white that shows in the ground of a check or stripe, the dressier the shirting.

Different collar styles also connote varying degrees of dress-up. Spread collars are generally dressier than straight point collars and become even more so with each degree of openness. White contrast collars elevate the formality of any dress shirt regardless of its fabric's pattern or color. As such, it should be worn only with a French cuff in either self fabric or contrasting white. However, much like a button cuff on a white contrast-collar dress shirt, the straight point collar in contrasting white is a bit of a sartorial oxymoron. Contrast-collar dress shirts look less authentically classy with collars whose points are not open enough to support their dressier intentions. Tab, pinned, or eyelet collars can likewise give a dress shirt a more decorous look. However, if you see a blue oxford dress shirt sporting a white spread collar or a button-down loitering on a dressy white ground English striping, avoid these mongrel offerings, for their questionable propriety will do nothing for yours.

Most of the criteria for purchasing a classically styled dress shirt have little to do with price or even the quality of the fabric. If a relatively inexpensive shirt made with a mediocre fabric has a collar that is flattering to your face and affords you the right fit, it will render greater value to you than a more expensively made shirt with the wrong shaped collar. Value has everything to do with longevity of wear, as ultimately, the most expensive clothes a man can purchase are those that rarely make it out of the closet.

SHOES

No single article of clothing is so articulate as a shoe, and none is so revealing of the status and attitude of the wearer. For a man, buying business footwear is often an act requiring considerably more time and thought than that given to the selection of an accessory or, for some, even a suit. The result must satisfy not only the wearer's aesthetic needs, it must also provide long-lasting comfort. Particularly for dress-up, any decision concerning men's footwear pivots on something of a paradox: the more imagination and taste one tries to inject into the choice, the more subtle the outcome should be. In terms of fit, strict attention is required, since shoes that are found to be unsatisfactory after several wearings cannot be altered like a suit of clothes. Therefore, purchasing a pair of shoes is a deliberate, thought-provoking act. I guess that's why *Esquire*'s legendary fashion journalist George Frazier said, "Wanna know if a guy is well-dressed? Look down."

Before considering a new pair of shoes, a man must first decide which sensibility of footwear fashion best complements his own dressing style. There are essentially three mentalities of shoe fashion from which to choose: Italian, English, or contemporary. As with tailored clothing, no matter how well made or costly the shoe, its longevity will be ultimately determined by its shape. The finest crocodile slip-on will be less desirable if, as your tastes change, you feel it makes your foot look too Cinderellaesque in contrast to your fuller-cut, pleated trousers.

THE CLASSIC ITALIAN SHOE

In reaction to the shapeless, Ivy League gray-flannel bags of the 1950s and their accompanying gunboat-shaped lace-ups, the style-conscious American became enamored of the body-hugging silhouette worn by the Continental sophisticate. Accordingly, slim-fitting Italian footwear, with its leaner lines and light construction, gained popularity. Its slightly pointier, slipper-shaped toe and close-trimmed soles attached to its small-pored, shiny-soft calfskin upper made the wearer's foot appear smaller than it actually was. The shoe's diminutive platform was the proper conclusion for the era's tapering, narrow-legged trousers.

THE CLASSIC ITALIAN SHOE: ITS LOWER LINES MAKE THE FOOT APPEAR SMALLER.

The fuller-cut clothing of the designer-driven 1990s, however, demanded a larger-scaled shoe. So nowadays, classic Italian footwear is divided into two design sensibilities: the Northern Italian preference for English bespoke-inspired larger-scaled lace-ups or dress slip-ons and the Southern Italian shorter-vamp, lighter-weight holdovers from the Continental era. This shinier, sharper look continues as part of the conservative Euro-classicism that still equates style with clothing that makes you look trim.

THE ENGLISH BENCH-MADE SHOE

The father of the post-boot, ready-made gentleman's town shoe is the bench-made English oxford. Once the straps were removed from men's breeches and the low-cut shoe replaced the boot, men's footwear was freed to pursue new expressions of design. Just as Savile Row artisans posted the benchmark for tailored fashion, West End cobblers set the international standards for high-class foot fashion. Most of today's British ready-made shoe designs were originally made during the period between the world wars for the custom-shoe trade. Although the British models and shapes have changed minimally since their intro-

THE TRADITIONAL BRITISH SHOE: ITS WELT CONSTRUCTION GIVES IT A MORE SUBSTANTIAL PROPORTION.

duction some ninety years ago, this footwear's upper-class lineage makes them the choice of the wellborn and well-bred to this day.

Since ready-made English shoes, like the boots and other military-style footwear from which they evolved, were created to endure cold, wet climates, their construction is stiffer and more durable than the lighter-weight footwear of the Mediterranean male. The English shoe uses a heavier leather on the upper, which is first stitched to a welt, a separate piece of leather. Then its leather sole is sewn to the welt of the upper. Heavier in look and feel than its Latin cousin, it offers superior support for the foot and body while providing considerable protection against the elements. Since its welted sole can be easily replaced without disturbing the shape of its upper, it will wear longer than the lightweight Italian product whose sole is either sewn or glued directly to the insole. When bench-made and hand-polished to an antique veneer, this article of English craftsmanship, like a fine set of luggage, looks and feels better with age.

THE CONTEMPORARY DRESS SHOE

This third, more modern fashion sensibility in footwear style evolved from two separate but parallel movements in men's fashion. In the early seventies the bohemian antifash-

THE CONTEMPORARY DRESS
SHOE: ITS LARGER SCALE
BALANCES THE FULLER CUT OF
MODERN CLOTHES.

ion crowd plucked the cowboy boot from its working environment and taught it a new rhetoric. Having then seen it usurped and cosmeticized by the hipper urban bourgeois, they switched to the more aggressive semiotics of worker-style footwear, adopting either the construction boot, the black high-laced American combat boot, or, the epitome of downtown chic, the Doc Martens mechanic's boot. Along with athletic shoes, which were beginning to be worn as much for leisure as for sport, these shoes all shared a street fashion insouciance as well as a new, larger scale of proportion.

At the same time, the world of high fashion witnessed the emergence of the Japanese kimono-inspired minimalist fashion along with Giorgio Armani's broad-shouldered slouch. Both expressions were fuller on top and required something different on the bottom extremities. Black space shoes such as Doc Martens addressed these requirements, as did any shoe from the past whose scale refused to be over-whelmed underneath all this sartorial largesse. The American CIA-issue black wingtips of the fifties, with their gunboat proportions, as well as some older European walking and country shoes, were adopted and became the precursors to this newest category of footwear design.

Today, every fashion designer or contemporary shoe

manufacturer has some of these larger-scaled shoddings as part of their collection. In addition, just as the slouchy silhouette was giving way to its slimmed-down, fitted fashion update, shoe designers proposed something entirely out of the box, or, in this case, a boxy tomb-shaped dress shoe, which is still being offered today.

The artifice of this latest footwear design seemed to appeal to those men whose feel for fashion was or is in the early developmental stage, much like those enthusiasts of an earlier decade who were seduced by the equally naïve vogue for the matching necktie and dress shirt. Unfortunately, a shoe with an exaggeratedly blunt, squared-off toe box violates a fundamental criterion of long-term style. Clothes whose lines deviate from or do not follow those of the body find themselves sharing permanent closet time with other casualties of premature obsolescence, such as the overly wide-shouldered jacket or flared dress trouser. And in this case, coming on the heels of the newest suit silhouette's sleeker, more fitted body lines, artificially proportioned footwear's fashion cycle is likely to be compressed that much further.

On the upside, what has started to emerge in part from this particular footwear shortfall is a confluence of shoemaking influences that has propelled a more refined version of the box-toed shoe to the forefront of the well-heeled's attention. First introduced to the high-toned Bond Street set back in the early postwar years by legendary English cobbler George Cleverley, and more recently popularized by the business expansion of the famous Paris *bottier* Berluti, the elongating, chiseled square toe of the bespoken world has insinuated itself in the ready-to-wear firmament. And what better shape of toe to extend the sharper, more defined lines of the newest designer suit silhouette than the subtle, refined lines of the sheathlike, chiseled-toe dress shoe.

FITTING THE SHOE

The greatest challenge to a proper shoe fit rests in the very nature of the foot. Though it might not be immediately obvious, your foot's shape and size are not static. They change depending on the time of day or season, the prevailing climate, and whether your foot is at rest or bearing the weight of your body. Adapting a somewhat fixed object (the shoe last) to one in constant flux (the foot) requires fine design and skilled technology. All of the factors that theoretically govern proper fit can be present, but in the final analysis, it's the customer who determines whether the shoe does or does not fit, and this is a wholly subjective decision.

Size alone is not a determining factor. Five different pairs of feet may possess identical measurements, but when fitted in the same shoe style and size each may react differently. Toe shape can have an impact on size and fit; materials—such as cordovan, which has little yield, or calfskin, which has greater stretch—are another important consideration. However, the first thing you must determine when trying on a shoe is whether its last is appropriate to your foot.

The last is the wooden form around which the shoe is constructed and the form the leather adopts once it is on your foot. John Lobb, the famous London bootmaker, titled his book *The Last Comes First*, and that's as true today as it ever was. Shoes of the same size but made on different lasts will offer dissimilar fits. All shoes, from custom-made to mass-produced, must start with a sculpted wooden last. Any discomfort from the heel, the instep, the ball of the shoe, or its toe are determined by this wood carving. This ready-made form must approximate the shape and character of your feet so that the shoe becomes like a second skin after several wearings.

Shoes should feel comfortable from the moment you try them on. Certainly, they will feel better with wear, but comfort should not be deferred if the fit feels wrong within your first few steps. If shopping for a dress shoe, make sure the socks you are wearing are the same weight as those you would normally wear with this shoe; fitting a lace-up shoe over athletic socks could prove counterproductive. Shop in the afternoon rather than in the morning, as your feet tend to swell during the course of a day's activity.

Take the time to have your feet measured properly. Most people believe their feet are smaller than they actually are. A well-trained shoe salesman should always want to measure your feet first rather than ask you your size. Never buy expensive shoes from a salesman who does not know how to take a proper measurement. And since studies show that only 15 percent of all men have a right and left foot of exactly equal size, you should insist on having both feet measured. After trying on both shoes and putting them through some paces, sit down for a minute before walking in them again. Let your feet settle. Two pairs of feet can have similar measurements while at rest but register distinctly different numbers after bearing weight.

If the shoe in question is a lace-up, you should be able to tie the laces so that there is no more than a quarter-inch gap between the opposing edges at the top. Slip-ons can occasionally be bought one half size smaller than a lace-up, which means only a $3/16$-inch difference in length and mass. A lace-up is cut higher up the instep so it stays on the foot more easily, while a slip-on is cut lower and needs to stretch and collapse more. Boots, athletic shoes, and casual shoes are better bought a half size larger than your other shoes, since they are usually worn with thicker socks and your feet tend to perspire more due to their encasement. Also, since they usually must endure harder wear, your feet will need greater room to expand.

It is difficult to identify all the criteria that justify the price of expensive shoes, but one of these is certainly the construction of the shoe's interior, which should be finished as meticulously as its outside. It should be fully leather-lined with leather insoles, since no material is better suited to absorb all the moisture produced by the foot while making a substantial contribution to the shoe's continuing shapeliness and comfort.

Better shoes also have leather heels, sometimes tipped with rubber for better wear. Leather heels retain their shape when exposed to the elements. The heels of most less-expensive shoes are made with a resinlike hardboard which will splay out when wet, losing their shape and support. The stitching that attaches the sole to the upper on top-quality shoes is buried in a groove that cannot be seen by the naked eye. On less expensive shoes, the stitching is exposed and erodes quickly with wear.

FOOTWEAR DECORUM

While black shoes are predictably correct for dark navy suits and formal wear, brown actually offers a man more stylish flexibility. Notice how any article placed on a polished mahogany tabletop immediately acquires an expensive aura. Based on a similar dynamic, top-quality brown leather shoes confer a richness and character to any type or color of fabric worn in close proximity.

Boston Brahmins have long appreciated the eccentric classiness of mating brown lace-ups with navy or charcoal suits. Today's best-dressed group of men, the Milanese, are almost religious in their preference for brown footwear over black. Their saddle-tanned business shoes are bone-polished to a deep, dark patina while their rubber-soled brown suede weekend shoes are reserved for less postured leisure wear.

Murray Pearlstein, proprietor and dean of America's most enlightened men's fashion store, Louis, Boston, spent most of the 1980s spreading the brown shoe gospel.

While the English may shudder at what they consider to be a perversion of their established form for town wear, I seem to recall one of their own, the future Edward VIII, donning his brown suedes with a gray chalk-stripe lounge suit back in the 1920s, setting a sartorial precedent and a new tradition all in the same Long Island afternoon. Though it's been some time since Edward VIII set his crowd abuzz, dark brown suede tie shoes are finally coming into their own as an alternative business shoe for men desiring to step out with a little more chic. Long misconstrued as a foppish affectation of the "look *anglais*," the brown suede shoe is now being worn and appreciated by the younger tie-and-jacket-wearing denizens.

Like a hand-rolled white linen handkerchief peeking out of the breast pocket of a tailored jacket, this footwear makes anything worn with it appear more expensive and smart. These shoes look good with clothing of any type or color and, owing to their break with traditional shiny-surfaced footwear, represent something of a departure for the arriviste fashion consumer. But, once familiar with its aristocratic heritage, you will find that no shoe adds a more cultured swagger to a man's tailored ensemble than the dark brown, reverse-calf suede lace-up in its most town-elegant model—the semibrogue with perforated cap toe.

It's difficult to explain why other colors such as burgundy, navy, or dark gray have never connoted much class or taste in masculine footwear. Perhaps it's because shiny, dyed colors appear artificial next to the more natural saddle-leather colors of brown and black. The only time color in male footwear escapes being viewed as stylishly sophomoric is in the nonreflective, napped surfaces of suede or velvet found in such status-conferring classics as the Gucci buckled slip-on, Belgian loafer, or Prince Albert dress slipper. In these models and fabrics, dark colors such as bottle green, burgundy, navy, or chocolate brown come off as refined, not contrived.

A similar principle applies to white as a color for summer shoes. The red-soled English white buck has a definite blue-blooded American cachet, as do the two-tone correspondent shoes that made their debut in this country as leisure wear during the 1920s. But if the white suede of the correspondence shoe has been replaced with shiny white leather, as it is in most of today's commercial versions, it's a horse, *ahem*, of a different color. Representing an era when the care of high-maintenance attire was left to those employed to look after the privileged, authentic two-toned shoes are as difficult to maintain as they are to polish. However, substituting leather for white suede renounces the shoe's wellborn origins and reduces its taste from the patrician to the parvenu.

HOSIERY

Most men consider hosiery a necessary staple, but one hardly worth the expenditure of much thought or money. Completely concealed when standing, mostly obscured when walking or sitting, no part of a man's ensemble is likely to elicit less notice. Those men who pay more than just casual attention to this stepchild of an accessory do so primarily for their own private enjoyment.

However, at the risk of boring the socks off you by making the first of many references to those legendary toffs of yesteryear swank, Fred, the Duke & Co., these men selected their ankle adornments with the same care and eye for personal expression they brought to the rest of their attire. Hosiery is yet another element that a man can use to enrich his ensemble. Doing something interesting with your hosiery is just one more opportunity to cultivate your own taste and, in this case, should you fail, few will be the wiser.

Socks are chosen by the clothing and shoe company they will keep. As a general principle, the dressier the outfit, the finer the hose. The choices range from sheer silk for formal wear to fine-gauge wool or cotton lisle for business attire to wool argyles, cotton cables, or ragg socks for casual wear. Just as a navy cotton cable sock would appear too sportive under a dressy pinstripe worsted business suit, one would not mate a pair of semisheer lisle hose with a rough tweed jacket and flannel trousers.

The most egregious breach of hosiery etiquette that a man can commit is to allow a patch of skin to show between trouser and hose while seated, because his socks are too short. The chances of such a faux pas occurring today have been significantly minimized with the introduction of over-the-calf dress hosiery. Garters have gone the way of separate collars, and ankle-height hose is now only available in sport socks. Although garters (or suspenders, as the English call them) sound Victorian, when made well and worn correctly, they are comfortable and do not require the corseting of the entire leg up to the knee, as over-the-calf hose does.

Since the foot is almost completely encased by some form of covering, natural-fiber hosiery has always been the choice of those who are willing to invest the time required for its proper care. Nothing makes a man feel more sure-footed and confident than the feel of fine-gauge 100 percent natural wool, cotton, or linen hose caressing his foot as it is massaged by the supple leather lining of a well-crafted dress shoe. And since the shoe is subject to constant moisture, heat, and friction, nothing contributes more to better foot health than absorbent, air-circulating, natural-fiber hose.

ANKLE DECOR

The function of ankle outfitting somewhat parallels the role of the belt in relation to the shirt above it and the trouser below it. When chosen well, a waist wrapping should meld the two while embellishing the visual transition. As with the dress belt, the darker the sock, the dressier the effect. Conversely, the lighter or brighter the stripe of expanse between trouser and shoe, the more casual the look.

A sock should match the trouser rather than the shoe. Footwear and hosiery that work as a unit ultimately appear to separate themselves from the whole, instead of functioning as an extension of it. With a navy suit and black shoes, navy socks look richer than black. With a dark gray suit and brown shoes, charcoal gray hose is the more elegant choice. While de rigueur for formal wear and obligatory for the downtown folk swathed in regulation black, solid black hose should be avoided for business wear; it transforms the ankle into a black hole and diminishes that which it could beautify.

The next step up in trouser cuff decor is the adoption of a third color that echoes one found in any of the accessories above the waistline. With a dark gray suit, medium blue dress shirt, and navy and wine tie, one might consider burgundy hose, whose dark coloring aids the transition from trouser to shoe while subtly incorporating this area of the ensemble into the whole. The prize for the most soigné of modern ankle veneer must go to the Milanese, who will anoint their charcoal suit trouser and dark brown brogues with bottle green hose, reminding the observer that their choice of a dark green necktie was no accident.

Socks sporting a two- or three-color design or decorated with a clock bring you to the playing field of the hall of famers. This is where hosiery acquisition becomes considerably more focused, as only ankle knitwear of real character can make the team. Scoring here imparts the same sense of freedom one feels once he becomes comfortable wearing a patterned necktie with a patterned dress shirt. If you start your exploration with such time-honored combinations as two-toned houndstooth hose with glen plaid flannels, fine herringbones with striped suitings, or spaced polka dots with windowpane worsteds, donning your socks in the morning will no longer be routine.

Acquiring truly handsome hosiery poses a serious challenge for those who cannot afford to spend at least twenty dollars for a pair of socks. While technology has extended the life of this once perishable accessory, it has also homogenized the designs found in the mass market. Pre–World War II hosiery was not made to last more than a dozen wearings, so it was inexpensive and designed to encourage impulse buying, like neckwear. Once nylon and other synthetic fibers were introduced, resulting in the one-size-fits-all dress sock, the days of sized hosiery with creative designs were numbered. The new high-speed knitting machinery must produce megavolumes to pay for itself and has changed hosiery from a specialized commodity into a mass-produced wearable. Fortunately, Europe is still capable of turning out high-quality sized hosiery with some real style and character.

With most retailers preferring to carry only stretch socks and most men not even knowing their true size, other than the more expensive European sized hose, it is one predictable world of dress ankle fashion. In the States, Bergdorf Goodman, Barneys, and Paul Stuart in New York City stock the best imports, while each major city hosts the odd specialty store, which usually stocks a smattering of imported sized hose. Of the designer hosiery currently being offered, Ralph Lauren's is by far the most elegant of the commercially made one-size.

However, with dress-down fashion gaining wider acceptance around the world, casual hosiery is flourishing and, with it, many appealing, chunkier foot cushionings. As this area allows for greater texture and fiber combinations, the hose have a much greater range of design possibilities. Here, the one-size-fits-all sock provides comfort, function, and fashion when worn under the larger, less-than-exact-fitting athletic shoe or walking boot. Since such footwear usually covers the entire ankle, this hosiery can be provocative and colorful—only you and a select few will ever see them.

Unless the economies of producing elegant hose change in the near future, sized hosiery will go the way of the exact-sleeved dress shirt. It will virtually disappear for those who cannot afford to pay its higher price. If you do come across some sized vestiges of a previous time like hand-clocked lisle hose, patterned wool hose, hand-knitted cables, or real Scottish argyles or bird's-eyes, like a collectible, buy as many of them as you can afford and squirrel them away for some special future occasions.

Neckwear:
Icon of Western Culture

This adjunct to male elegance once carried more information about its wearer than any other item in his wardrobe. Whereas a man's suit told you something of his present position, the necktie—be it of the club, old school, regimental, or wedding variety—was usually a reliable chronicler of his past. It could speak volumes about his breeding, education, or social station. Unfortunately, the go-go fashions of the eighties transformed the tie's traditional role as harmonizer into an ornament of surfeit. However, with the tailored-clothing market reflecting the current decade's increasingly sober and less grandiloquent mood, the neckwear aesthetic is once again in transition—searching for a more mannered yet modern expression.

Fortunately for the necktie, its fortunes seem to improve in tougher economic times. The go-go eighties and bull markets of the new century's first decade witnessed an increasing casualization of the corporate landscape. As businesses thrived, the necktie's presence dipped, almost disappearing from the office and boardroom. However, with the world economy in recent freefall and business uncertainty and job insecurity suddenly rearing their heads, the times have demanded a more traditional businesslike appearance. Rebound the necktie and its sartorial affiliates, the business suit and dress shirt.

Today, it is increasingly common to see men in positions of authority without a necktie. With business attire no longer fettered by strict social codes, casual dress now shares the office with the tailored uniform. However, when power and success need to be communicated, no ensemble delivers such a message more poignantly than the well-tailored Business Suit & Co. While men may be wearing fewer suits and neckties to work, on those occasions where full-tilt corporate attire is required, many men have upgraded their sartorial firepower to the best quality vestments they can afford. As a result, dressy full-bodied wovens and prints along with all manner of highbrow four-in-hands have now returned from virtual fashion obscurity to the forefront of corporate style.

Advising a man on how to choose a stylish necktie is like helping him pick one that makes him feel handsome—the final decision is that subjective and personal. Ideally, the necktie should be a strong indicator of the taste and style of its wearer. Yet despite its potential for conveying the wearer's individuality, it's no longer clear who the modern necktie speaks for. Sixty percent of all men's neckties are purchased by women. Bill Blass, one of America's preeminent taste makers, once observed, "A woman should not play too large of a role in the clothes a man wears. Men who have learned to mix patterns have mastered something very important. Since a tie is one of the best forms of self-expression a man has, why should his wife pick it?"

I not only endorse that sentiment, I would go even further: it is virtually impossible for a man to dress well if he does not select his own clothing. With few exceptions, sophisticated dressers—be they men or women—rarely trust their wardrobe choices to a second party, no matter how respected or beloved that person might be. The man who aspires to cultivate a feel for stylish neckwear must be willing to immerse himself in the trial-and-error process of its screening selection. A man can learn as much from a failed purchase—the tie that looked so smart in the shop but now rarely escapes his closet—as he can from one he cannot stop wearing. Confidence comes from being able to make the right decision, not having it made for you.

PERMANENT NECKWEAR FASHION

Some neckwear designs transcend the caprices of fashion. Like a well-cut gray flannel suit, these ties retain their stylishness by virtue of their incontestable good taste. With the four-in-hand reclaiming its rightful role as the refiner of its surroundings, sumptuous is again the order of the day as the woven necktie with its unparalleled richness of hand rises to the top of the barrel. Ties of all woven textures from satin to faille to grenadine have returned. Small Macclesfield wovens such as black-and-white shepherd's checks or silver wedding ties and simple two- or three-color geometrics preside as the classiest neckwear known to spread-collared gents.

DIAGONAL GEOMETRY OF STRIPED NECKWEAR CHISELS AWAY BOTH BREADTH AND SOFTNESS FROM THE FACE.

Woven stripes have found their place under the well-furnished chin. The smarter dresser will notice how their diagonal composition magically chisels away breadth and softness from the face. While the settings are less regimentally British, the direction of their stripes should indicate their English heritage. Following the jacket's left over right fastening, they should run from the left shoulder down toward the right pocket. Ninety years ago, when Brooks Brothers first introduced English repp ties to America, they cut them in the other direction (running from high right to lower left) to distinguish them from the stripes of the British club ties, which, technically, were to be worn by members only. This violation of sartorial dogma remains a point of contention between "striped blades" from either side of the herring pond.

Print ties should likewise feel sumptuous to the hand. The better ones use more expensive silk print cloths whose weight does not need the artificial puffing up of a thick interlining. The finest quality foulards, like those of Hermès, use more silk cloth in their construction, which produces a superior hand and a better knotting and longer lasting necktie. Designs such as the impeccably civilized polka dot or two-color geometric, appropriately modernized in scale and setting, have made their way into the well-heeled closet.

The new, modern, sexier designer silhouette with its emphasis on clean, sleek lines will likely spawn an interest in solid color neckwear of all persuasions, starting with the ne plus ultra of four-in-hand chic, the Cary Grant–favored solid silk satin in rich navy, black, medium blue, or garnet. And as cloths with greater surface interest become more acceptable in tailored clothing, neckwear will respond in kind by bringing back the textured neckties of cashmere and silk for winter's tweeds along with the spongy, linenlike silks for summer's nubbier jacketings and mohair-blended worsted tropicals.

JUDGING A NECKTIE'S VALUE

The price of a fine necktie today can range wildly from $75 to $250. Many of the criteria formerly relied on to identify the quality and degree of a necktie's hand crafting can no longer be discerned by the average consumer. Establishing the tie's relative value used to be a straightforward affair. However, modern technology has produced machines capa-

ble of simulating hand-stitching with such verisimilitude
that the results can deceive even the trained eye. Additionally, the designer business has dramatically altered the relationship between value and price. Under its standard, the
article's visual composition—rather than the inherent quality of the tie's shell fabric or craftsmanship—becomes the
primary benchmark for valuation.

Today, the perceived status conferred by the tie's label
and the design of its shell fabric constitute the major factors
governing its purchase. Given how easily technology can
feign a product's pedigree and that the allure of most neckties is grounded in their surface design, the average consumer must often rely on a store's reputation or the knowledge
of a salesman to accurately judge its value. Frequently it is
the individual shopkeeper who sets a particular standard of
quality whether his customers demand it or not. For example,
Hermès uses more silk in its neckties than other printed
foulard makers, while, for example, the Alan Flusser custom
shop sells only the most expensively crafted neckwear. If in
doubt, ask the salesman to justify the tie's higher price by
pointing out its virtues, such as whether it is completely
handmade, self-tipped, and so on. If no one in the shop is
able to do this, and such considerations are important to
you, find a store that knows more about its product.

Thoughtful books on neckwear recommend a number
of tests that can be performed by the prospective buyer to
verify a tie's workmanship. You can hold the necktie suspended in front of you by its narrow blade to make sure it
doesn't twist. This confirms it was made correctly and cut
precisely on a forty-five-degree bias. Or you can verify a tie's
resiliency by gently pulling it from both ends to see if it returns to its original shape. There are some other paces to
put a tie through that years ago might have had some rele-
vance to this discussion but needn't be mentioned here. I

have subjected ties from high-quality stores or manufacturers to enough trials to conclude that for every tie that passed
each of these inspections, I found another from the same
source that did not. If, after knotting the tie, it was still to
my liking, I would buy it anyway.

In my opinion, the only reliable gauge of a necktie's
quality and value is the consumer's sense of feel. As you
touch a tie's surface, your fingers must immediately respond
to the sumptuousness of its outer fabric. Gently pressing
down on it, you should detect the lush cushioning provided
by its inner construction. Of these two main ingredients,
the tie's most tangible asset, its outer shell, accounts for
two-thirds of its price. A costly tie should possess a rich
and sensuous "hand." This term describes a fabric's tactile
character—its weight, texture, and fall. All fine ties are
made of 100 percent silk. No other fiber produces a fabric so
densely soft or as capable of reflecting light so richly. The
best silk for neckwear is woven or printed in Italy and England, though a few excellent examples can be also be found
from France and Switzerland.

Ties must absorb a lot of pressure, especially in their
knotting areas. Looking fresh and hanging straight when
worn, uncreasing and returning to its original shape after
wear, and resisting the ravages of continual knotting are the
function not only of the tie's outer fabric but, more important, of its invisible interior. For the same reasons a tailored
jacket's collar and armhole function better and last longer
when hand-sewn, no wearable allows for more give than
those sewn together by hand. Fine neckwear is either made
completely by hand or by machine with hand-finishing. A
skilled artisan can produce around ten handmade ties per
hour, while the hand-finished process can turn out several
thousand in a day. In the 1970s, the Liba machine was
invented to close the envelope of the tie. It has now been

refined to such a degree that it can actually replicate the irregular slip stitches of the handmade tie. Even many seasoned manufacturers cannot spot the difference without taking apart the tie.

The one constant characteristic of a better-made tie is that it comes in three sections, while cheaper ones are composed of two. Many ties are tipped with a fancy acetate that is a dead ringer for silk. The resemblance is so close, asking the salesman is often the only way to tell the two fabrics apart. The best ties, of course, are tipped with real silk. However, there are two easily detected details of construction that, if either is present, immediately justify the tie's expense.

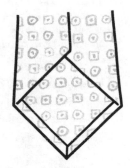

SELF-TIPPING: A TIE WHOSE BLADES ARE FINISHED WITH THE SAME FABRIC AS THE SHELL IS A COSTLY PRODUCT.

Since both require costly labor, it is assumed that no maker would risk such an investment unless the necktie's shell fabric could also command a higher price. If you turn over the tie's apron or blades and find they are tipped with the same material as the shell rather than the customary lightweight synthetic tipping, it is the product of a costly process. This self-tipping, or French tipping, as it was formerly termed, requires more of the outer shell's expensive silk.

On less expensive ties, the label is sewn on the back side of the front apron as a keeper of the narrower rear blade. Some better ties use the tie's own fabric for this self-loop, which certainly looks more refined and finished. However, the finest neckties go one step further by tucking the self-loop's ends into the blade's center seam, thereby anchoring it securely and insuring it will not pull out with wear (see page 66). If the tie you are examining has either of these

SELF-LOOP: IF A TIE'S BACK LOOP IS TUCKED INTO THE CENTER SEAM OF THE TIE'S LARGER BLADE, IT IS AN EXPENSIVELY MADE NECKTIE.

telltale ingredients, you are in the presence of neckwear art and should be prepared to pay accordingly.

The ultimate in neckwear craft is the seven-fold tie which, as its name indicates, is a silk square folded by skilled hands seven times to produce a cravat of matchless luxury. It has no lining other than its own silk. There are probably no more than four or five makers of this handiwork left in the entire world. This is distinctive haberdashery for true aficionados and you should expect to pay at least $175 for such an indulgence.

HOW TO WEAR A TIE

Whereas a tie's color or pattern represents the signature of its maker or designer, how it is worn says something unique about its wearer. The only step in a man's daily dressing ritual usually performed with the aid of a mirror is the knotting of his cravat and its positioning up into the shirt collar. Over time, performing this male rite should become another manifestation of personal style. However, given the frequency and repetition of this daily habit, it's amazing how few men understand how a tie should appear when correctly set in a dress shirt collar.

Military officers are taught a dress line. This vertical line bisects the chin, continues down the middle of the collar and tie, passes through mid–belt buckle, and finishes at the tips of the shoes. This image offers a good guideline to follow when suiting up in a dress shirt and tie. When a dress shirt collar meets to form an upside-down V and is filled by a tight, purposely made knot whose dimple extends this imaginary downward line, the composition emanates subliminal authority. President Obama does this particularly well.

If the tie is not pulled up smartly into the collar and arched out a bit from the neck, the power of the entire arrangement becomes diluted. This is why serious practitioners of tie comportment often opt for tab or pin collars. The added support these collars afford keeps a tie standing at attention throughout the day with a minimum of periodic fixing.

AUTHORITY IS CONFERRED IF A VERTICAL LINE PASSES THROUGH THE CHIN, THE COLLAR'S UPSIDE-DOWN V, AND THE TIE KNOT'S DIMPLE.

KNOTTING THE TIE

The knots most men construct are usually hand-me-downs from their fathers. Although two knots—the Windsor and half Windsor—still enjoy limited usage, it is the four-in-hand that remains the knot of preference for most elegantly attired men. Not only is it the simplest knot to execute, it fits better into the average dress shirt collar than any other knot.

The larger, triangular Windsor knot was originally introduced to fill the opening created by the spread collar's horizontally angled points. Also, fuller-faced men felt this wider knot looked better under their large chins. Unfortunately, unless you wear a rather high-banded

THE NECKTIE SHOULD BE PULLED UP INTO THE COLLAR SO THAT IT IS TIGHT ENOUGH TO ARCH OUT SLIGHTLY FROM THE NECK.

spread collar with longer points, the Windsor knot tends to lift the average collar points from the shirt's body. Sophisticated dressers also find its look much too self-conscious. The

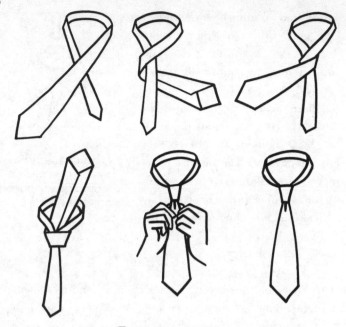

TYING A FOUR-IN-HAND.

four-in-hand, with its conical and slightly asymmetrical shape, is infinitely more stylish. The half Windsor might be excused, if only to give a thin tie a fuller knot. If your tie needs to have a larger knot, use the Prince Albert version, which basically loops over a second time. This produces a larger, cylindrical knot which can fit into more collars than the broader Windsors.

No matter which knot you prefer, never buy a tie whose bulk or texture will prevent it from being able to be smartly pulled up into the collar. Some knit ties or wool ties can make too large a knot if they are not designed properly. When in doubt, always knot them in the store to see how they sit in your collar. In fact, never purchase any brand of neckwear you are unfamiliar with, without knotting it up first.

A tie's proportions should relate to your jacket lapels and shirt collar. Traditionally, the ideal width of a man's necktie was guided by the width of his jacket's lapels, which in turn were determined by the breadth of his shoulders. A man with narrow shoulders has less chest to drape a lapel across, therefore the lapel's narrower dimensions dictate a narrower width tie. Conversely, a broad-shouldered man requires the scale of a more generous lapel and thus a wider width necktie. As a general guideline, keeping a tie's width between 3¼ inches and 3¾ inches for suits up to size 44 will put to rest any fears that fashion may one day render it obsolete. However, for the new contemporary, slimmer fit designer suit silhouette featuring narrower lines all around, tie widths can retreat to between 3 inches and 3¼ inches to better harmonize with its smaller proportions.

Though it may be acceptable in England, a tie's length should not be seen falling below the waistband of your trousers. If your tie is too long, tuck the offending excess into your pants in the style of Fred Astaire or the Duke of Windsor. Its bottom will get wrinkled, but if it's always worn this way, it can only offend your closet. Tie bars are an excellent way to keep the tie from flying about and look better worn angled slightly downward. Wearing a necktie with a bar or tucked into the trousers will also keep it out of the soup while helping to maintain its arch in the shirt collar.

THE BOW TIE

Wearing a bow tie has never been an issue of fashion. Its adherents often wear them to signal their contempt for such a perceived insecurity. By implying that its wearer is a man of independent thought, the bow tie conspicuously separates him from the conformity of the necktied pack. However, the

THE BOW'S WIDTH SHOULD
FINISH WITHIN THE OUTER
EDGES OF A MAN'S EYES
AND THE OUTSIDE LINES OF
HIS COLLAR.

BOW TIES THAT EXTEND
BEYOND THE WIDTH OF THE
WEARER'S FACE OR COLLAR
MAKE HIM APPEAR GIFT-
WRAPPED.

bow tie's identification as a formal accessory has done much to create mistrust in its use as everyday wear. Bow ties can be worn for all occasions and are appropriate with either single- or double-breasted jackets.

A bow tie should not appear to overwhelm its shirt collar. As with other neckwear, a bow tie needs to be framed by the collar. Reverse that perspective and you appear swathed. A slightly larger-scaled collar better offsets the bow's horizontal geometry. Collars such as Brooks Brothers' fuller-roll button-down, longer straight point collars, or semispreads with some degree of softness all help frame the tie's irregular bow.

To wear a bow tie stylishly, two elements must be considered. First, its width should not extend beyond the outer edge of a person's eyes or the breadth of his collar, whichever is wider. If it violates these borders, a man will appear festooned no matter how elegantly the bow is tied. And how it is tied is the second, more important issue.

As with a four-in-hand, there is no reason to consider wearing a bow tie unless you plan on tying it yourself. Place a pretied model under your chin and you forsake any claim to individuality or style. It's like allowing someone to forge your signature. The lines may be exact, but where are the moody loops and unpredictable swirls that declare it com-

pletely yours? A bow tie's style, especially its unmanufac-
tured imperfection, rests on its celebration of the individual.
A too-perfectly-knotted bow tie looks prepackaged, measured, and ready to squirt.

Bow ties assume two basic shapes: the thistle and the
narrower bat's wing. Though they can be worn interchange-
ably, the thistle end should not exceed 2¾ inches or be less
than 2¼ inches. And the bat's wing can range between 1½
inches and 2 inches. Just as braces used to be sold in exact
lengths, bow ties were formerly available in exact neck sizes.
This made it nearly impossible to purchase one which finished in a bow whose width was too broad to fit the wearer's
face, unless it was by choice.

Today, most bow ties come in adjustable sizes. Therefore, never buy a bow tie without first trying it on. You
should always be certain how it looks tied and if its width
can be altered by reducing the neck size. If your neck size is
16, you can always set your bow tie one half size smaller.
This maintains the bow's width on the smaller size—the side
to err on when in doubt. Some bow tie ends are so long, no
amount of downsizing will render a proper fit.

With black-tie wear as the exception, avoid woven
designs and concentrate on printed foulards when formu-
lating your daytime bow tie collection. Like printed pocket
squares, less formal bows need softness and malleability if
they are to come off looking unaffectedly natural. However, striped bows should be of woven silk, otherwise they
lose some of their schooled authenticity. In printed foulards, look for polka dots, newer geometrics, or any pattern
that has some movement in its design. And remember, like
a fine felt fedora, the bow will avoid looking like a point of
exclamation only if its style resides within its manipulated
imperfection.

KNOTTING THE BOW TIE

Learning to tie your bow tie is not the daunting task you might imagine; it requires the same skill most men had to master when they were taught to tie their shoes. First, sit down and cross your legs. Wrap the tie around your thigh just above the knee. Hold one end of the tie in each hand. Close your eyes and tie the bow as you would your shoe laces. Opening your eyes, you should find that, though it may lack a certain aesthetic, you have tied the bow into a recognizable knot.

With the tie still wrapped about your knee, you can begin to fine-tune the bow. Hold its left loop in your left hand and its right loop in your right. Pulling the two sides in opposite directions will tighten the knot while pulling the tab ends will reshape and straighten the loops. Even though the bow tie may look delicate, you will learn how solid its

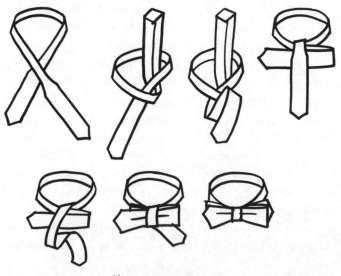

KNOTTING THE BOW TIE.

knot becomes and find it will remain so until it is untied. After familiarizing yourself with this process, replicate it in front of a mirror while still shirtless. A shirt collar only complicates the learning process for a novice (see diagram). You may have to repeat this exercise several times, but don't be frustrated. Once learned, tying a bow tie is like riding a bike.

ACCESSORIES:
BELTS AND BRACES,
JEWELRY, HANDKERCHIEFS

BELTS AND BRACES

During the 1920s, the height of male elegance, most gentlemen sported braces (an English invention and term), since most suits were worn with vests, and belts added yet another unnecessary layer of bulk around the waist. During the Victorian era suspenders had been held in the same regard as underwear. With the emergence of the two-piece suit, they became exposed to public view—a sign of poor breeding. As a result, belts gained acceptance for business wear and found an unqualified reception by the burgeoning sportswear market.

Braces fell further into disuse as men accustomed themselves to belts during World War II and continued to wear them in ever increasing numbers throughout the gray-flannel era of the 1950s. As the waistline slipped to the hips during the peacock era of the sixties through mid-seventies, the fortunes of suspenders experienced a similar descent. Tight-fitting low-rise trousers and hip-hugging jeans kept suspenders as the private province of the Savile Row dresser and East Coast WASP.

It was not until the early 1980s that fashion's fuller-cut clothes returned the trouser to the natural waistline. In the mid-eighties, the blockbuster movie *Wall Street* featured Michael Douglas as Gordon Gekko, donning suspenders for his high-octane character. Braces began to win back a little of their own. However, with the ascendance of the slouchier,

Armani-inspired dress, their popularity again waned. Today, the lower-rise, belted trouser style of the modern designer suit has, once again, relegated braces to those haberdashery-prone aficionados who prefer their trousers to drape from the waist in the old-fashioned, time-honored way.

Originally a brace, like a belt, was made in exact sizes so that its back fork and adjustable front levers could be appropriately positioned according to the wearer's height. Its levers were supposed to rest in the hollow created by the protuberance of the chest and the taper of the waistline. If set above the bottom half of the chest, not only would the levers' double layer of ribbon bulk up the chest, but their gilded buckles would be distractingly close to the wearer's face. Today, most braces are sold in only one size, so the majority of them are cut to accommodate taller men, leaving shorter men with their suspenders' levers resting up around their necks. If your braces are so cut, ask the store to have them shortened. If they cannot accommodate you, take them to a shoe repair shop that has the machinery to do the job properly.

THE BRASS LEVERS SHOULD REST IN THE HOLLOW BETWEEN THE PROTUBERANCE OF THE CHEST AND THE TAPER OF THE WAISTLINE.

THE POSITIONING OF THE SUSPENDER TAB DIRECTLY OVER THE FIRST PLEAT IS ESSENTIAL TO CONTROL ITS OPENING AND MAINTAIN TENSION ON THE TROUSER'S FRONT CREASE.

The front buttons inside the suspended trouser's waistband should be directly in line with the main pleat closest to the fly. This not only helps the pleat to lie smoothly when standing, it also defines the trouser's crease and anchors its depth. Buttons set too far to the side of the trouser reduce the pressure on the shoulder strap, making it likely to slip from the shoulder.

For the record, few clothing or brace manufacturers use properly shaped brace buttons. Ideally, when attached to the waistband, they should permit enough space for the brace's leather loop to move freely from side to side. Originally, during the era of vested suits, braces attached to domed buttons on the outside of the trouser waistband. Most brace buttons today are so flat that attaching the suspender's loop to the trouser becomes more difficult than necessary as well as limiting the loop's freedom of movement.

BRACES OVER BELTS

1. The waist expands when you sit and returns to its smaller circumference on standing. The looser-fitting suspended trousers accommodate these changes in stomach dimensions. Belted trousers can fit comfortably in only one position or the other.
2. Braces encourage better posture. You can suck in that gut and jut out that chest without fear of losing your trousers.
3. With braces, you can set the desired length of the trouser in the morning, then never have to bother with them for the rest of the day. Belted trousers, fitted as they are to one precise length, tend to slip down to the hip and require more attention.
4. Pleated trousers drape better suspended rather than belted. Set on the natural waist and above the horizontal tug of the hips, their pleats remain defined and move gracefully in concert with the leg.
5. Unless a man's front is washboard flat, belts tend to push the stomach out, spreading the pleat unnecessarily.
6. Even more than a necktie, braces allow the wearer the

option of injecting a bit of his own personality into the visual fray.

7. The extension waistband of a braced trouser is more simple and thus more refined than that punctuated by a belt buckle.

Belts over Braces

1. Many men regard the wearing of braces as too much of a cultural cliché, too readily assigning them to a particular social background or business path. Belts are stylistically neutral and leave more of the wearer to be revealed at his own discretion.

2. Men who wear their trousers on their hips or under their stomachs cannot do so comfortably while wearing suspenders.

3. Brace straps can easily slip off men with sloped shoulders.

4. Many men believe that the belt and buckle appear sexier to women.

5. In summer, when the body perspires more, a man becomes increasingly conscious of the straps lying on his torso, even though the space between the body and the suspended trouser permits more air to circulate. Historically, it was during those warmer months that men started experimenting with belts.

Buying the Suspender

Today, the finest suspenders are made of rayon, replacing yesteryear's silk. The straps are cut in 1¼-inch or 1½-inch strips. Any smaller and they will bind; any wider and they will feel cumbersome and unnatural. Never buy braces with clip ends or in an elastic fabric unless you are also planning to purchase a farm. Avoid braces made with necktie silk that is backed for reinforcement, as they are neither authentically stylish nor durable. Any design on the braces' straps should be woven into them rather than printed on the surface. Only woven designs possess the structure and character to convey this appurtenance's utilitarian lineage.

Top-quality suspenders come with leather fittings and adjustable brass levers. England's Albert Thurston can still turn out the Rolls-Royce of brace construction, while America's Trafalgar makes a lighter-weight brace with top-quality fittings as well. The knitted ends seen frequently today were originally favored for evening wear, since their softer, pliable ends felt less bulky under a waistcoat or cummerbund. Their colored ends relieve one from adhering to the conventional protocol of matching this leather detail with the color of the shoe.

If the store is prepared to pay a premium, Thurston will still make hand-stitched white leather ends (as opposed to the original white catgut, which is too difficult and expensive to craft) that will eventually turn yellow. Since most Englishmen adhere to black for town footwear, the white catgut was always preferred for the brace's leather trim. However, in an effort to hold down prices, white, black, or brown machine-made ends have been introduced. But, like the working buttonholes on custom-made jacket sleeves, if you want to trump the hoi polloi, the old-fashioned white catgut earns the connoisseur's nod.

Since braces share the same vertical plane as the tie, their coordination is primarily guided by their relationship to each other and only secondarily to the dress shirt and trouser. The sophisticated dresser demonstrates his sartorial faculties by using the lines of the brace to frame the composition of the furnishings. Solid or striped braces achieve this objective with more versatility and ease than patterned ones. As most men's neckwear tends to be patterned, the solid or

striped ribbon can pick up one of the colors without conflict-
ing with the tie's design. Patterned braces, on the other
hand, are easier to coordinate with a solid or striped necktie.

Buying and Wearing the Dress Belt

Not only should the dress belt's exterior be made of a fine-
grain leather, its underside should also be leather-lined.
When buckled, its end should be long enough to finish
through the trouser's first belt loop, but not so long as to run
past the second. Its width should vary between 1¼ inches
and 1½ inches. The dress belt's color should conform to the
ensemble's other visible leather element, the shoe. This usually eliminates most hues except those that are shades of
brown or black. Buckles should be sturdy but simple, in
brass or silver, depending on the color of your jewelry.

Dress belts should be darker than the suits they are
worn with. The darker and finer the leather, the dressier
the belt. Lighter-hued leathers set against the backdrop of a
darker trouser convey a sportier nuance, as does a rougher-
grained or more textured leather. Crocodile and lizard constitute the luxury end of the dress belt spectrum. As the
Boston Brahmins have long known and the Northern Italians have recently affirmed, mating brown shoes with any
traditionally colored business suiting ranks a smidgen above
the predictable black on the sophistication scale. As brown
shoes are going to be more frequently seen in the company of
dark suits, you would be well advised to consider investing
in the finest brown crocodile belt affordable.

HANDKERCHIEFS

Since the close of the fourteenth century, when the English
monarch Richard II declared it boorish to blow one's nose

on either one's sleeve or the floor, the use of a handkerchief has been considered a symbol of gentility and social rank. The lineage of the navy blue blazer may in part be credited to this desire to impose a higher standard of propriety among those in service to the crown. As legend has it, the captain of the HMS *Blazer*—in anticipation of a visit from Her Majesty Queen Victoria—outfitted his crew in navy serge jackets to smarten their appearance and affixed rows of brass buttons on their sleeves to discourage them from wiping their noses on their all too visible sleeves.

Immediate availability has always been a requirement for any handkerchief; the user must have ready access to it if he is to head off that unexpected sneeze before it becomes a source of embarrassment, mop up the spilled champagne before it flows into the lap of a guest, or perform other social niceties. During World War I, officers cached their handkerchiefs within their coat sleeves, in deference to their uniform's hard-to-open buttoned-down or flapped pockets. Soon after, the one for "blow" was tucked safely away in the unflapped rear trouser pocket, while the dress handkerchief, the one for "show," returned to its rightful place, the breast pocket. All properly designed tailored jackets have such a pocket, appropriately angled to better contain and set off the breast handkerchief. As no serious writer would want to compromise his prose by omitting the correct punctuation, no serious *élégant* leaves his chest pocket similarly unattended.

As with the adaptation of like artifacts of sartorial polish—French cuffs, collar bars, braces, and so forth—the donning of a chest handkerchief is an act of dressing up and finish. As such, it is an enterprise that most men avoid like some plague, fearing that they will do it incorrectly, badly, or both. To the less sophisticated it can smack of the effete and precious. This is unfortunate, since the inclusion of a simply folded white linen handkerchief into a suit jacket's chest pocket is the simplest and least expensive way to give a mediocre suit the aplomb and distinction of a more expensive one.

Complicating the question as to whether the omission of such an elitist trapping equates to a lack of stylish propriety is its philosophical conflict with today's ethic of minimalism as it equates to dressing. The pared-back simplicity and monotone rigor favored by current fashion thinking are undermined by the inclusion of such a high-contrast embellishment. The problem could be sidestepped by lowering and angling the chest pocket's position and filling it with dark-toned, less high-contrast pocket squares, thus bringing it more into the whole. But for now, since that thought represents a fashion that may never materialize, I will confine this discussion to the guidelines as set down in the heyday of breast pocket fashion—the 1920s and 1930s—when no man could consider himself a practitioner of fine dress having not yet come to terms with the minor art of rigging out the breast pocket.

One would be hard-pressed to find a picture of the Duke of Windsor, Fred Astaire, or Gary Cooper in which some form of pocket square is not in evidence. For each of these Promethean dressers, the breast pocket afforded yet another opportunity to express his own style. While the Duke of Windsor's linen hanks were always neatly folded, they were worn at odd angles and in unconventional positions in the pocket opening. Gary Cooper's were less self-consciously folded, looking as if he had only just stuffed it in a few seconds before greeting you and possessing the same unstudiedness as his curled-up dress shirt collars. Fred Astaire liked to wear his silk squares in a puff fold he allegedly invented. Wearing a handkerchief that looks neither affected nor sloppy is akin to developing a discerning palate for good wine or food; it takes some practice. Douglas Fairbanks Jr. often reminded me that if you want to dress well, it takes time to look as if it took no time at all.

Dressing the Breast Pocket

In order to purchase a pocket handkerchief wisely, you should know beforehand how you plan to wear it and what colors you expect it to meld with. Pocket decor is but one element of an entire composition. It should not be used as an exclamation point or function as one end of a parenthetical bracket (with the other end being the tie). The observing eye should never be encouraged to travel horizontally across the wearer's body. Overtly coordinating, or even worse, matching the tie and handkerchief, is a sure sign of an unsure dresser.

Pocket handkerchiefs are harmonized on two bases: color and texture. If a solid handkerchief is chosen, its color should echo one color in the tie's design, provided it is a multicolored pattern. If the pocket square is patterned, one color of its design should match or, at a minimum, complement the dominant color in the solid or two-color tie. When wearing a multicolored pocket square, it is simplest to keep to a solid tie or simple two-color stripe with more ground than stripe. Use one of the hank's colors to reflect the primary color of the tie. If particularly skilled, you can use the remaining hues to pull in the shirt and suit.

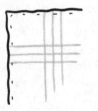

A FINE HANDKERCHIEF'S EDGES ARE ALWAYS HAND-ROLLED.

To play down any contrivance, the textures of the tie and pocket square should also differ. Once you accept this dictum, the too-common practice of wearing a tie with matching pocket square becomes a nonoption. If the tie has a silken luster, the pocket square should be of a dry material such as linen. If the tie is of a dulled fabric such as wool, linen, or cotton, the pocket square can be shiny, such as a printed solid or foulard.

Only in certain cases would it be considered in good

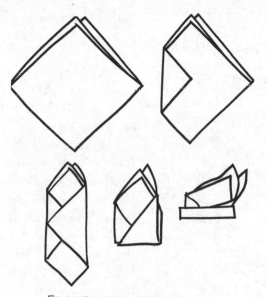

FOLDING A LINEN POCKET SQUARE.

taste to make the pocket square your ensemble's focal point. Dressy high-contrast ensembles such as navy and white for daytime or black and white for dinner wear can support the exclamation point of a brightly colored silk pocket square. This style works well so long as it is not forced to compete with another component for center stage, thereby breaking up the ensemble's symmetry into too many pieces.

Like the subtle hand-stitched edge of a finely tailored jacket lapel, a fine-quality handkerchief always has its edges rolled by hand. Since the linen handkerchief is folded to reveal its points, the edges need the graceful roll and stitch of handiwork to properly convey its refinement. The starchier linen hank produces a dressier look than the jauntier, printed foulard. The best size for a pocket handkerchief is the sixteen- to eighteen-inch square, with the printed silk foulard lightweight enough to hold its fold without bulking up

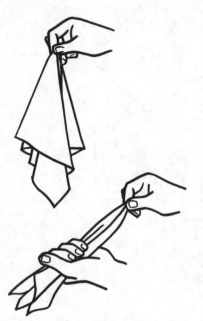

FOLDING A PRINTED
SILK SQUARE.

the pocket. When considering a printed foulard, first try it folded in your pocket to see if it either bulges excessively or drops out of sight from lack of substance. The silks require a bit of careful technique so they can project a natural and un-fussy aplomb. Whether folded with points showing or in some version of the puff fold for silk pocket squares, the handker-chief should be angled toward the shoulder. This positioning helps in fostering a dégagé air, while emphasizing the lapel's diagonal slant and shoulders' breadth.

JEWELRY

Some wearables cannot be classified as clothes, but with-out them many men would not feel completely dressed. In pre–World War II days, a hip flask and cigarette case were considered essential accessories for a generation that believed a drink before and a cigarette after were two of the three best things in life. The demon-ization of tobacco has stigma-tized even the most stylish of smoking implements, while the flask has gone the way of the swizzle stick. For the moment, sex is still in fashion.

Since Victorian times, men have tended to avoid all but the most discreet and functional of decorative accessories. The 1980s—that decade of "affluent fashion"—revived those few sanctioned items of male self-embellishment that could succinctly communicate the wearer's business and social status. With the return of cuff links, suspenders, the collector's watch, and select writing instruments came a proliferation of shops specializing in such paraphernalia. The eighties saw more men become collectors of vintage jewelry and watches than in any other period of the twentieth century.

The golden age of jewelry workmanship spanned the mid-nineteenth century to the outbreak of World War I, with the Art Nouveau and Art Deco periods also producing some extraordinary design and craftsmanship. Today, sporting a pair of Edwardian cuff links or an early Cartier tank watch affords men one of the few opportunities to actually wear an ornament of beauty and antiquity without incurring the suspicion of his confreres. Being able to recount some fanciful but true anecdote explaining the item's origin, or recalling its first (and, ideally, celebrated) owner only enhances this collectible's secondhand mystique.

It's been said that watching a man undo his cuff links is every bit as sensual as hearing the zipper slide down the back of a woman's dress. While I cannot comment on the first part of that observation, one thing that I can state unequivocally is that no form of shirtsleeve closure dresses a man's hand better than a well-fitted French cuff punctuated by the subtle glamour of its buttonhole-covering link.

The most prized examples of antique cuff art have always relied on all four faces to convey their craftsmanship and lineage. To fully exploit the cuff link's decorative potential, each side should bear a design and be conjoined by a link or chain—the reason it is so named. Wearing a set that clips on one side not only exposes its superstructure, but suggests you could afford to pay only for the gold or gemstone on the outside. Though it is a bit easier to link your French cuffs with a bar that pushes through its four buttonholes, you end up dressing only half of each hand.

Cuff links with stones, even colored ones such as rubies, emeralds, or sapphires, were traditionally frowned upon as daywear and usually reserved for black tie as part of a set of studs with matching links. In the light of day, such a display would still be considered somewhat ostentatious, although they can certainly be worn after dark to accompany a dressy business suit. An antique set of studs is another acquisition to consider seriously. Like owning a fine pocket or dress watch, having something different for formal occasions endows the ensemble with its own specialness and creates an heirloom that can be passed down to a son or beloved nephew in a rite of passage.

Another implement of elegance adopted by many knowledgeably dressed men is the gold safety pin, used to pull up a soft straight point or rounded collar into a dressier pose. Like the tab collar arrangement, this joining of the collar keeps the necktie arched and in place all day long. If the shirt is a better one made with cotton linings, the pinholes will disappear with washing. The gold pin should never be worn with a shirt whose collar has eyelet holes. This type of collar requires a bar with two balls (or some other shape) on either side, one of which unscrews to permit proper fastening. I've seen a few of the more swanky embellish their collar tackle by adding cabochon sapphires or small rubies to either end of the bar or pin. Avoid modern collar slides; most of them do not have sufficient spring in their mechanisms to hold the collar without slipping during the course of an active day and, as they generally tend to be too long, fail to pull in the collar sufficiently. However, if you come across one from a previous age when they were better constructed, test it with a tie done up in the collar. If it holds, snatch it up, as they are very rare.

Tie clasps, an American invention, can add a touch of controlled flourish. They should be bars of understated design neither large nor gaudy, although should you come across a whimsical one this is not a bad place to affect a little highbrow humor. The bars keep your tie from substituting as a napkin while helping the tie remain arched in the neckband. They also add a measure of panache for those shorter men who choose to tuck their ties into their belt lines à la Fred Astaire, who loved tie bars and high-waisted trousers. The aficionados angle theirs downward to affect a less posed air.

As for finger regalia, the simpler the better. More ornate nonmarital finger decorations are associated with men who make a living by commission. Signet rings are an elegant alternative to the simple wedding band or jeweler's ring. When engraved with the wearer's initials, they suggest one hails from the gentrified side of the tracks with forebears who might have used theirs to seal correspondence or parcel out land.

Fortunately, we have gone beyond the Victorian notion that deemed the public display of a timepiece vulgar, since a true gentleman's concerns were not supposed to include the passage of time. On the other hand (pun definitely intended), the actor Peter O'Toole may be carrying things too far when he wears watches on both arms simultaneously. When queried on an American talk show why the double dip, he replied, "Life is too short to risk wasting precious seconds glancing at the wrong wrist."

Early decorum required the pocket watch to accompany the tailcoat, while a slim dress watch was acceptable for dinner clothes or dressy day wear. Wearing a Dick Tracy–scaled timepiece with a dressy suit not only contravenes the aesthetic principle of form following function, it is also guaranteed to expedite the fraying of the shirt cuff. Gianni Agnelli, chairman of Fiat and Italy's own Duke of Windsor, resolved this problem in his own maverick manner by wearing it over the cuff. On him it looks aristocratically idiosyncratic; on most others, it looks contrived. Watches should be chosen to smarten the hand, not encumber it. When it comes to keeping time fashionably, as with most men's jewelry, less is usually more.

FORMAL WEAR

If a man's suit ranks as the most articulate garment in the language of clothes, then his formal wear should guarantee sartorial eloquence. Due to the ritual surrounding the way it is worn and what accompanies it, formal wear's original spirit has been relatively well preserved. The simple combination of richly textured black accented by fresh white contrasts bespeaks refinement. And so it is that this last vestige of upper-class attire continues to live on in the dinner jacket, with its comforting certainty that all men look good in it.

Acquiring high-pedigree dinner clothes represents one of the more difficult challenges facing today's male consumer. That is not because, as with neckwear or sportswear, its variety can overwhelm one; rather it is because high-toned dinner clothes are difficult to find at any price. Much of what is represented today as "black-tie" is the store's or manufacturer's judgment on how much of a difference from his normal business attire the average man is prepared to accept in his dinner clothes. This applies not only to commercially produced tuxedos, but to the majority of expensively hand-tailored ones offered in fine specialty stores as well. In some cases, straying from the archetype is motivated by cost. Tailoring the properly detailed tuxedo requires particular trimmings and therefore more labor. Often, however, its lack of pedigree is a function of simple ignorance resulting from not having been sufficiently exposed to the genuine article.

In spite of male evening clothes being highly formulaic and regimented by their very nature, opportunities to observe this particular masculine attire being worn correctly today are surprisingly rare. Menswear designers offer their alternative buttoned-up and casual versions each season, while the Hollywood celebrity typically engages a "stylist" to make sure he looks fashionable. While most of the concoctions are motivated by trying to modernize or individualize the formal ensemble, the resulting confections usually turn out to be something less than transcendently stylish.

For example, the current vogue for substituting a dark suit and long tie for the real McCoy suggests not only the wearer's sartorial insecurity, but also his susceptibility to fashion conformity. If a man's formal wear is supposed to set a higher style standard than his day clothes, and it is, then dressing down to dress up contravenes both the form's logic and its function. Proposed as an alternative way to defang the predictable and ordered bow-tie-trimmed tuxedo, this latest fashion contrivance has now morphed into exactly what its sponsors were trying to avoid, a look-alike regiment that imposes a predictable homogeneity to all practitioners. The irony is that if men could return to wearing a tuxedo as it was originally intended to look, they would appear not only more suavely turned out than their long-tie-wearing brethren, but more individual.

The fact is that many men go to considerable effort to look special in a tuxedo when to do so is simply a matter of knowing what constitutes high-class formal wear and how it's supposed to look on them. A man's formal attire should be neither formulaic nor cultish. Unfortunately, that which separates the classic from the commonplace is almost an extinct knowledge of the form's original design principles, which have long transfigured average men into movie stars—okay, make that the Adolphe Menjou variety.

I feel that before one attempts to improvise in the ceremonial world of men's evening attire, it's important to understand the original design's intention and aesthetic logic. Trying to improve upon its ordered predictability in an effort to achieve a more personal expression is to be encouraged. But to create something unique and stylish, one should base such decisions on practical knowledge, rather than personal opinion or ephemeral fashion.

Since the culmination of the dinner jacket's final format in the late 1930s, nothing has improved upon the genius of its line or the refined aesthetics of its component furnishings. This does not mean that to own a fine tuxedo, one must have it cut or even tailored like those from the tuxedo's heyday. It does mean that its modeling and detailing must respect the exquisite relationship of form and function that were worked out through the collaboration of English tailors and shirtmakers with their fastidiously dressed customers of that stylish era. No other period could have produced such a success, because each step of the new form's evolution was being compared to and measured by the perfection of the outfit it was intended to replace, the granddaddy of male refinement, the evening tailcoat and white tie. Not only did the tuxedo's final form end up projecting the same level of stature and class as its starched progenitor, it did so while providing considerably more comfort.

I will introduce briefly the dinner jacket's unusual history and its relationship to the tailcoat-and-white-tie ensemble, so that we may apply its rationale to selecting proper dinner clothes today. As W. Fowler said in his 1902 book, *Matter of Manners*, "The man who knows what to avoid is already the owner of style."

THE HISTORY OF THE DINNER JACKET

BLACK TIE, TUXEDO

As the name suggests, the original dinner jacket was to be exactly that, a less formal dining ensemble for use exclusively in the privacy of one's home or club. The original design was created during the mid-nineteenth century for the English prince who later became Edward VII. He decided there should be a comfortable alternative to the constricting swallowtail evening coat and bone-hard white-tie getup worn at the dinner table. The consensus is that the very first model of this shortened jacket must have been a rolled collar (shawl) double-breasted lounge suit in black worsted with grosgrain facings. The same design in velvet was worn as a smoking jacket by gentlemen at home, its grosgrain facings lifted from that of the tailcoat's lapels. Victorian ladies did not smoke and insisted any husband who did should confine this activity to his den. The smoking jacket could then be left there, in situ, so as not to radiate the noxious fumes around the rest of the house.

Edward's dinner jacket was admired by the husband of an American houseguest visiting him at Sandringham, his country estate, and the man asked the prince if he could copy it. Edward consented and the American brought the innovation back to his millionaires' club in Tuxedo Park, New York. In 1886, one Griswald Lorillard, sporting his version at the club's autumn ball, scandalized his hostess and hastened his departure, but forever established the jacket's place alongside the tailcoat-and-white-tie ensemble.

From that point in the late nineteenth century up through the early days of the 1920s known as the golden age of the British gentleman, black-tie attire continued as an option at home or in a men's club. However, for an evening in public, white-tie remained the dress of choice by polite society. The 1920s produced menswear's first unofficial designer, the new arbiter of fashion, David, the Prince of Wales, who was later crowned as Edward VIII but is better known by the title he took after his 1936 abdication, the Duke of Windsor. Clothes-conscious and a bit of a maverick, he was determined to throw off the stuffy formality of his father's generation of court-ruled attire and make clothes more comfortable for himself and his fellow aristocrats.

The prince often arrived for dinner in dinner coat and black tie when everyone else was decked out in full tails. Sometimes he would wear a lounge-coat-like double-breasted dinner jacket with silk facings on the lapels or he would take the piqué dress vest from the tailcoat outfit and wear it with a single-breasted dinner jacket. Before giving up the throne, he abdicated the boiled-front evening shirt and its separate stiff wing collar, replacing them with a soft, pleated-front dinner shirt and its attached soft turndown collar. He devised a backless waistcoat with lapels to wear in warmer climes. Although he was not the first to wear it, he helped popularize midnight blue for dinner clothes, which by artificial light looked richer than black. By the end of the 1930s, with his international coterie of friends adopting such elegant comfort in public, the dinner jacket, an amalgam of the tailcoat and lounge suit, began to replace the swallowtail dress coat and white tie.

WHITE TIE AND TAILS

The king of all male civilian garments is the evening tailcoat. Its long tails confer dignity while its starched white expanse of piqué waistcoat, shirt, and tie flatters even the most rubicund of faces. The evening tailcoat has changed very little in the two hundred years since it was a riding coat. Its major alteration occurred when its double-breasted

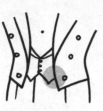

THE PIQUÉ WAISTCOAT'S
POINTS SHOULD NEVER
EXTEND BELOW THOSE
OF THE TAILCOAT.

THE CORRECT BACK
LENGTH OF A TAILCOAT
SHOULD LINE UP WITH THE
BACK OF A MAN'S KNEE.

model was altered so it no longer buttoned in front. The single-breasted cutaway retained the button stance from the double-breasted model, as it does today. The outfit was, and still is, pretty straightforward, entailing very little choice in either color or detail. All that was needed was to tailor its established proportions to the wearer's frame, and presto: its debonair magic turned average men into movie stars.

The outfit consisted of a white piqué bow tie and matching stiff white piqué-front evening shirt with attachable wing collar, worn with a single- or double-breasted piqué vest, black worsted swallowtail coat, and matching trousers trimmed with two rows of braids on the outside of each leg. Black silk hose worn under patent leather oxfords or opera pumps with grosgrain bows completed the uniform. A white linen handkerchief with hand-rolled edges graced the breast pocket, while a colored carnation as boutonniere was optional. The only dressing errors egregious enough to scuttle its perfection were if the waistcoat's points extended below those of the tailcoat's front (a common occurrence today) or if the length of the coat's tails were not resting exactly in line with the back of the man's knees.

The White-Tie Evening Shirt

The piqué-front evening shirt had a separate stiff wing collar whose shape evolved from turning down the corners of a stiff stock that was worn with a starched cravat, a nineteenth-century Beau Brummell fashion. The white piqué bow tie was made to exact neck sizes, so that in addition to covering the exposed metal head of the front and back collar studs, the bow's intended width was fixed.

The wing collar sat high under the chin, giving extraordinary stature and definition to the face and chin. Its high back was to show ¾ inch above the jacket's collar, or ¼ inch higher than the black-tie's more comfortable turndown collar. The collar's wings helped to keep the piqué bow in place by pressing it forward. The angle of the opening and height of the collar determined the style and size of the bow tie. The outer edges of the bow never finished outside the edges of the wing collar. This boilerplate guide for all bow-tie wear was established during that time and is respected even today.

PHOTOGRAPH BY ROBERTO DUTESCO

Complementing the wing collar, the evening shirt's sleeves took single, stiff cuffs that, like the collar's height, were intended to show more than the softer French-style double cuffs of the black-tie dress shirt. The "boiled" shirt-front look took one or two studs, and the type of stud fastener determined the size and shape of the opening through which it connected with the stud's head, thus covering any evidence of the shirt's construction. The shirt's bosom, a biblike design in stiff linen or piqué, was to fit so that its width did not extend under the trouser's suspenders, and its length was to stop short of the trouser's waistband. Because of its stiff front, if you sat down without it being secured to the trouser, it would billow out like a sail in full wind. A tab with buttonhole affixed the shirt to a special button in the trouser's waistband, keeping it in place and worry-free.

For all of this arithmetic to add up, the dress trouser needed to fit on the natural waist and not below it. This was accomplished with the help of suspenders (termed "braces" in the King's English). Without a high-waisted fit, the vest would not cover the bottom part of the shirt's bib and have its points finish above those of the tailcoat. With all of these studs, straps, and buttons needing to be in their proper places, putting on the white-tie ensemble might appear to be a form of Victorian bondage. In fact, when the clothes were tailored correctly, they were both comfortable to wear and moved in graceful concert with the wearer.

Most of these designs were transformed and worked into the classic tuxedo's final composition. Thus the stiff white-tie and "boiled" shirtfront gave way to the black-tie's softer lines without compromising its formal look, and so on. Keeping in mind the design heritage one searches for when selecting a tuxedo, let's move on and consider this information as it applies to today's black-tie dressing.

DINNER JACKET DOGMA—THE DETAILS

WEIGHT

Most formal affairs are held indoors, where central heating and air conditioning ensure comfortable temperatures. So most men prefer a fabric weight that provides comfort for more than a single season. Unfortunately, contrary to popular opinion, there is no such thing as a year-round weight;

no cloth can both warm you in the frost of winter and cool you in the heat of summer. However, a fine worsted cloth of nine to ten ounces will get one through most climate-controlled environments rather handsomely. Since most affairs include dancing and dining, when in doubt, err on the lighter side. While your dinner jacket may never drape like the gravity-prone, fourteen-ounce worsteds worn in the old movies, you should not have to suffer in pursuit of elegance either. If you wear a dinner jacket frequently enough to justify owning more than one, a choice of weights will certainly expand your style and comfort quotient. You could drop to a lighter, seven-and-a-half- or eight-ounce fabric for summer wear and move up to a fuller eleven- or twelve-ounce weight for fall and winter.

Model

A man of any size, shape, or weight can look stylish in a double-breasted tuxedo; it just depends on how it is cut. Both single- and double-breasted models are equally authentic and correct. The single-breasted model is worn unbuttoned, requiring its exposed waistband to be covered by a cummerbund or dress vest, and providing more opportunities for accessories and versatility. The double-breasted model relieves you of this additional layer around the waist, but the jacket looks better buttoned when the wearer is standing. Men tend to unbutton it when seated, so this model ends up being fussed with more than its single-breasted counterpart. A double-breasted dinner coat is never worn with a vest or cummerbund underneath.

Color

Black is the norm, while midnight blue with black trimmings is also worn. Midnight blue comes across less green and more rich in artificial light than black; however, such a garment is rarely offered in the ready-to-wear world. In America, between the beginning of the summer season, June 1, and the end of August, an off-white or tan-colored dinner jacket may be worn. On trips to the South or warmer climates, these light-colored jackets are perfectly acceptable throughout the year.

LAPELS

Only shawl or peaked lapels are used for dinner clothes. Peaked derives its heritage from the tailcoat, shawl from the smoking jacket. The shawl lapel produces a softer, old-world

THE PEAKED LAPEL IS THE MOST DRESSY DESIGN FOR DINNER JACKETS.

image and tends to be used on alternative tuxedo jackets such as the white summer dinner jacket, velvet smoking coat, or more idiosyncratic ones in wool tartan or cotton madras. Men with round faces or less muscular physiques generally look smarter in the uplifting, sharper-angled, pointed-end peaked lapel. Both lapels possess the sweep and self-importance that helps differentiate the black-tie coat from the less formal suit jacket.

THE SHAWL LAPEL IS ALSO CORRECT AND DEBONAIR.

A dinner jacket with notch lapels is a sartorial oxymoron, like sporting a dinner shirt with a button-down collar. (Actually, I've seen this done as a kind of tongue-in-cheek old-boy eccentricity.) Not only does this sportier coat lapel design lack the aesthetic logic and refinement required of formal wear, its casualness makes the rest of the ensemble look common and less dignified.

All dinner jacket lapels require a working buttonhole on the breast pocket side for a boutonniere. Many times, one finds himself in a wedding party or other official circumstances as an usher where he is asked to wear a flower. There is nothing more sophomoric-looking than having to pin one on the lapel. It makes this one flourish of tailcoat élan appear clownlike.

Custom-made dinner clothes pay even more attention to the buttonhole area by sewing a loop as a stem keeper under the lapel. You could ask the store if they could cut a buttonhole in the dinner jacket's lapel, although they will probably discourage you. It takes a qualified tailor to correctly determine its proper location and to execute a well-finished buttonhole through the silk-faced lapel. It is done all the time in custom clothes, however, and even if the buttonhole is machine-made, the boutonniere will cover it up. The buttonhole should be no less than one inch in length.

POCKETS

The tuxedo pocket must be dressy, yet simple. There is really only one type that should appear on the dinner jacket and that is the jetted or double besom pocket.

Besom pockets can be of self fabric, as on a dressy day suit, or trimmed in the lapel's silk facing. Flap pockets belong with notch lapels; neither were ever intended for formal clothes. While flap pockets are cheaper to

THE JETTED OR DOUBLE-BESOM DESIGN IS THE ONLY POCKET STYLE APPROPRIATE FOR A DINNER JACKET.

make (as are notch lapels), they also add a layer of cloth to the hip, and are thus neither slimming nor simple enough for such elegant apparel. Just as you would not expect to find peaked lapels on a tweed sports jacket or cuffs on dinner trousers, you should not see pocket flaps on a dinner jacket.

VENTS

The original dinner clothes were made ventless and then later offered with side vents. Ventless jackets are more slimming while side vents provide easier access to trouser pockets and are more comfortable to sit in, something one does a lot at formal occasions. Single vents are fine for horseback riding, as they open up, providing comfort while in the saddle. Unfortunately, they also open up when a man puts his hand in his coat or trouser pocket, exposing his back side as well as a patch of dress shirt. Single vents are acceptable on single-breasted coats, never on double-breasted ones, and with their sporting heritage, they compromise the intended formality of the tuxedo.

TRIMMINGS

Because grosgrain or ribbed silk was originally used on tailcoats, this style of trimming has always been considered a bit more refined than the shinier, more theatrical satin. In the early days of off-the-peg English tuxedos, many carried satin facings, so the ribbed silk came to be identified with the Savile Row–made tuxedo. The best facings are made of pure silk, while less expensive ones contain a synthetic component. Shawl lapels look fine in satin or grosgrain. Grosgrain facings permit some contrast in textures for the bow tie, while satin facings demand the bow tie to match which, especially if not hand-tied, will produce a more contrived effect.

The dinner jacket's buttons can be plain or covered in the lapel's facings. Some of the more old-world custom tailors cover their dress buttons in a fine, woven silk design, which at first may look a bit fancy, but can be quite subtle and distinguished. Like the tailcoat and better lounge suit, the jacket sleeves are to be finished with four buttons, their edges touching. Fewer buttons is not dressy enough, more is frivolous.

THE DINNER TROUSER

Pleated trousers are compatible with a cummerbund or waistcoat. Sitting is certainly a lot easier and more comfortable in pleated trousers than plain front. Their waistband must be covered, so they need to fit as high on the waist as is comfortable. Suspenders help to maintain their correct height, and keep their pleats lying flat under the waist covering. The side seams are trimmed with one band of facing (as opposed to white-tie, with two rows), which should conform in texture to the lapel facings—satin for satin, braided for grosgrain.

Dinner trouser pockets are usually cut on the side seam. Vertical pockets are dressier and easier to get to, especially if their top section is partially covered by a weskit or cummerbund. Better dress vests have side slits to facilitate pocket access. Dress trousers never take cuffs. How could they with their side-seam decoration? A wonderful depiction of this tradition can be enjoyed watching the Fred Astaire classic *Shall We Dance.* (For fit, see page 17.)

THE BLACK-TIE
DINNER TROUSER
CARRIES ONE STRIPE.

THE TAILCOAT
TROUSER REQUIRES
TWO STRIPES.

THE BLACK-TIE WAIST

Hardy Amies, the English tailor, would term it "naf or off," while the legendary English fashion journalist George Frazier would certainly sigh and complain it lacked any *duende* (style) at all. A trimmed waistband, as a substitute for a waistcoat or cummerbund, is thoroughly "bush league," to borrow a phrase from the days when this novelty was first introduced. Formal dress is ultimately about good form, and sometimes quick fixes that compromise such form need to be recognized as such and be avoided. The tailoring or finishing in high-class evening wear should be invisible, starting with the dress shirt's stud hole and extending to the trouser's waistband and side seam.

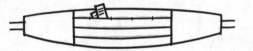

A CUMMERBUND'S FOLDS ALWAYS FACE UP
TO HOLD THE EVENING'S TICKETS.

While shawl-lapel dinner jackets look elegant with either form of waistband covering, the cummerbund's curved design harmonizes particularly well with this shape of lapel. A fine-quality cummerbund has a little pocket stitched behind its deepest pleat on the wearer's right side. This was to provide a handy and dignified place to keep theater or opera tickets at the ready, which explains why the cummerbund is always worn with its folds pointing upward. The single-breasted peaked-lapel jacket, like its sartorial antecedent, the evening tailcoat, synchronizes better with the dress waistcoat, as the vest's points below the waist echo those of the coat lapels worn above the waist.

THE BLACK-TIE DRESS SHIRT

The Collar

Two collar styles qualify as dignified enough to support the more formal design of the dinner jacket. The original, appropriated from the tailcoat ensemble, is the stiff wing collar. The second, introduced by the Duke of Windsor as a more comfortable alternative, is the attached semispread, turndown model.

Both collars do justice to any of the classic dinner jacket models, but of all the possible permutations, the one combination that tends to look better balanced is the wing collar with the single-breasted peaked-lapel dinner jacket. Again, its dramatic points are in perfect harmony with the coat's lapel design. Other than that particular combination, both collar styles are correct with either jacket or lapel style.

However, one of the more unfortunate casualties of the modernization of black-tie attire was the wing collar evening shirt. Its separate collar succeeded uniquely in framing and refining a man's face because of its stiff, high, wing design presentation of the bow tie. Once attached to the shirt, it began to be lowered and softened to fit a broader range of necks, and lost not only its stature but also its function. In spite of its resurgent popularity, today's wing collar evening shirts make most men look like mad scientists, as with one twist of the neck, their collar points crumble and roll over the bow tie. They have little height, no snap, miniature wings, and, not surprisingly, little presence. It's no wonder that ideas such as a banded collar evening shirt with a fancy button closure is being substituted. At least it offers a modicum of interest in an area where the drama of the wing collar would have formerly upstaged all the competition.

DINNER SHIRT DETAILS

The less dressy turndown collar dinner shirts usually have a soft pleated front. Sometimes they are made with a piqué

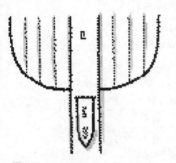

collar and matching front, called a Marcella dinner shirt. Since the wing collar dress shirt commanded a more severe formality, it took a stiff and simple front, either in piqué or starched cotton. Even though it is common to see today's wing collar mated with a soft, pleated front, it is yet another example of mixing sartorial metaphors—much like wearing a tassel loafer made from patent leather. All fine dinner shirts should be made with a bib-type construction so their fronts do not billow out of the trouser tops when seated. Bib

THE PROPER DINNER SHIRT IS CONSTRUCTED IN A BIB FRONT DESIGN SO AS NOT TO EXTEND UNDER THE TROUSER WAIST-BAND WITH A TAB TO SECURE IT TO THE TROUSER, SO THAT IT DOES NOT RIDE UP UNDER THE WAISTCOAT OR CUMMERBUND.

shirt fronts finish above the waistband and have a little tab that attaches to the trouser's inside waist button to keep it from pulling up. The width of the shirtfront should not extend under the wearer's suspenders. Wing collar shirts take one or two studs, turndown collars take two or three. Black-tie dinner shirts require a double or French cuff.

THE TUXEDO BOW TIE

The bow's color and texture are governed strictly by the jacket's lapel facings—satin for satin trimmings and a ribbed or pebble weave variation for grosgrain facings. Its thistle or bat's-wing shape is a matter of personal preference. The bow's width should not extend beyond the outside edges of the collar's wings or spread collar's perimeter (see page 70). Bow ties are always worn in front of the wing collar. The original collars were bone hard, and therefore it was impossible to place their parts over the bow.

Although the black-tie ensemble is a rather strict form of dress, its bow tie and pocket handkerchief offer some latitude for personal expression. They both look best done by hand, and a lack of perfection is desired, humanizing the ensemble and making it appear more individual. Most men cringe at the very thought of having to knot their own bow, but it is rare to find a stylish man who has not overcome that fear. It is one element of formal wear that continues to separate the skilled dresser from those who are content to let the form wear them.

FORMAL FOOTWEAR

The most aristocratic and elegant of all evening footwear is the black calf opera pump with black grosgrain bow. The man's pump, a word believed to derive from "pomp," is the oldest surviving vestige of nineteenth-century court fashion still in popular use. Originally worn in concert with silk stockings and silk knee breeches, its somewhat effete image accounts for its being misunderstood by the more macho contemporary dresser. Today it can be found only at Brooks Brothers, Polo Ralph Lauren, and Paul Stuart in Japan. Still the favorite of the connoisseur, its slipperlike club elegance bespeaks the unique character and upper-class heritage of black-tie attire. A more conventional alternative used to be a lace-up patent leather oxford (also more difficult to find), and in the correct shape, this shoe is quite classy in its own right.

The ideal ankle wrapping to augment all this polished swellegance is the black silk, over-the-calf or garter length hose with a self or contrasting clock design down either

side. The silk's dulled luster echoes the understated sheen of
the trouser's side braid while enriching the dulled matte
surface of the surrounding worsted trouser and black calf
shoe. The silk's surface also repeats the texture of the opera
pumps' grosgrain bow, adding the relief of illumination at
the end of a long stretch of dark black worsted.

COLLECTIBLE TUXEDO ACCESSORIES

In aspiring to make your formal attire appear less penguin-
like, it is very easy to end up gilding the lily rather than per-
sonalizing it. The idea is to accent the composition of black
and white with a single flourish of spice, a pinch of disso-
nance. The safest strategy is to replace one element in the
arrangement with either a third color or two-color pattern,
leaving the rest to keep the structure pulled together.

The best colors are those rich enough to hold their own
against the severity of black and white, such as bottle green,
burgundy, Vatican purple, deep gold, or dark red. If a pattern is chosen, it should be a recognizable classic such as
polka dot or houndstooth, or tattersall in two colors with
black as one of them (that is, black and red, black and gold,
or even just black and white). The ideal position for this dol-
lop of panache is where it can be surrounded by black and
thus integrated more into the whole. A vest, cummerbund,
dress shirt, and pocket square all have enough dark color
framing them to pull an alternative design into the composition. Some men choose patterned hose as their expression of
personal badinage, but that is best left to the more assured
dresser.

Less recommended, but by far the more practiced, is
the contrast bow tie. However, if the ensemble's only discor-
dant item is located directly under the chin, it ends up either
distracting from or competing with the desired focal point,

the wearer's face—something to be avoided at any level of formality.

Matched sets—such as bow ties and cummerbunds—should be shunned. The introduction of more than one contrasting accessory dilutes the form's symmetry, forcing the eye to move from one to another, thereby breaking down its whole into smaller, less important pieces. The black-tie ensemble is already regimented and predictable; adding coordinates that make you appear even more prepackaged not only suggests the wearer's lack of sophistication, but produces an effect of something more akin to gift wrapping. Proust said that elegance is never far away from simplicity, and that thought is especially applicable in accessorizing one's black-tie attire.

BLACK-TIE ALTERNATIVES
(TO BE USED ONE AT A TIME)

Dinner Jackets

1. Single- or double-breasted smoking jacket in black, bottle green, chocolate brown, burgundy velvet, or fine-wale corduroy with or without frog closings.
2. Black-watch tartan, printed silk foulard, madras, solid silk, in a single- or double-breasted shawl collar with self-facings.
3. For summer, off-white or Sahara tan, Panama weave, single- or double-breasted, self-faced shawl collar dinner jacket with midnight blue dress trousers.

Dinner Shirts

1. Spread-collar, pleated-front, high-count cotton or silk broadcloth in cream, medium blue, pink, or gold/yellow.

2. Any classically styled turndown collar dinner shirt in black and white color scheme such as gingham check, tartan, black polka dot on white ground, or striped black-and-white horizontal front.

FOOTWEAR

1. Black velvet Prince Albert slipper with embroidery or wearer's initials.
2. Black crocodile or lizard opera pump with black bow.
3. Black velvet patent-leather-trimmed Belgian dress slipper.

ALTERNATIVE ACCESSORIES

HANDKERCHIEFS

1. The finest hand-rolled white English, French, or Swiss linen handkerchief affordable.
2. Printed foulard in black ground with white motif in designs such as polka dot, tattersall, plaid, or other classic pattern. Its edges must be hand-rolled.
3. The above foulard in black/gold, black/dark green, black/red, or black/purple color combinations.
4. Hand-rolled linen or cotton in white ground with simple or fancy black border, black and white, check or plaid.

WAISTCOATS

1. The dress vest model should be single-breasted with shawl collar, three-button, full-back or backless construction. Better ones have an elastic loop for fastening to the trouser's front, and a longer back with vents on the sides.

2. Black ground silk foulard printed in paisley, polka dot, small plaid, or other elegant motif.

3. Small geometric Macclesfield woven design in black ground pattern. Fabric should have a slight sheen such as a dulled satin effect. Small figures, checks, paisley, repp stripe, or black moiré.

CUMMERBUNDS

1. The design should have a nice curve along its top line. Better ones come with an elastic loop for fastening to the trouser's front and a pocket for tickets.

2. Woven or printed designs in similar patterning to vest, with the folds worn up.

MODERN TUXEDO FASHION

If the invitation reads black-tie or black-tie optional, and the venue is a less formal one like a private dinner, theater party, or gallery opening, this would be the occasion where the more sartorially secure might consider taking some liberties in their formal attire. As such, it becomes a creative exercise whereby the tuxedo's ordered format is improvised upon by replacing generally one, or occasionally two, of its classic elements with a non-formal-wear wearable, however, one that possesses an equivalent level of timeless stylishness.

The most important item around which to construct any ensemble is the jacket. If designed and tailored well, it affords more options to dressing up or dressing down an outfit than any other kind of garment. In the case of alternative formal dressing, the most versatile tuxedo jacket is the black worsted, single-breasted peaked lapel jacket model trimmed in either silk satin or grosgrain.

The dinner jacket then becomes the glue connecting the old with the new, the classic with the eccentrically classic. Like the well-tailored vintage dinner jacket with its inherently transcendent stylishness, the properly designed dinner jacket can accommodate a wide range of accessories. Substituting a pair of blue jeans for the dinner trouser and teaming it up with a proper dinner shirt, black bow tie, and opera pumps becomes an outfit hip enough to wear for a downtown artist's black-tie opening. A simple black T-shirt or black H Bar C western shirt worn with black jeans and black velvet monogrammed slippers is another step down the less trodden but traversed fashion trail.

Or you could push the envelope in another direction by pairing black jeans with a horizontal black-and-white-striped dinner shirt, bow tie, and black Western boots (pointed toe and angled roping toe only). Let's not forget that black high-top Converse sneakers or champagne glass embroidered-type slippers are just a few of the alternative footwear that the urban sophisticate has been known to lob into the formal fray.

The late American fashion designer Geoffrey Beene adapted the Corbusier smock jacket, in various seasonal black fabrics, for his own formal outings. Its Mao-jacket lines are as timeless as the aforementioned men's tailored dinner jacket, and it functions as a neutral foundation to which personal elements can be added.

To dress in a modern way is to buy clothes that permit a maximum of accessorizing, clothes that convert from day to evening, dress to sport, inside to outside with the addition of one or two accessories. Develop an eye for the beyond-fashion classic. One man's oversized black cashmere cardigan sweater can be another's winter tuxedo jacket.

JEWELRY

This would be the right time to invest in an antique dress set, as it can be used for the rest of your life. The dress set should include shirt studs (two or three), cuff links, and three vest buttons. Though colored stones such as rubies, sapphires, and emeralds are discouraged for day wear, they can be worn in the evening. Black-and-white designs or simple gold always look refined. The perfect timepiece to accompany all this finery is a slim pocket watch, with an elegant cover and gold chain.

CUSTOM-MADE
CLOTHES

Wearing something created expressly for one's body and mind is an intoxicating luxury, particularly for men accustomed to buying off the rack. After realizing what such personalized raiment can do for him both physically and psychologically, it is the rare man who doesn't become a convert for life. Even in today's culture of instant gratification, a large majority of the world's best-dressed men still go to the effort and expense of having their clothes custom made. Bespoke fashion allows its wearer to act, in concert with whatever skilled craftsmen he has chosen, as the architect of his own look. This collaboration usually produces a dressing style that is individual and worldly.

Custom-made apparel is the product of exact measurements taken on a known individual. It's the difference between designing a garment on a real person and designing one for an imaginary figure. No ready-to-wear garment, no matter how well it is altered, can ever be as accurately fitted as one made by a skilled craftsman who constructs it right over the bones and bumps of his client. The maker must be an artist who can compensate for whatever nature has withheld. In cases where a considerable remolding of the client's form is required, the end result can become a glorified abstraction of the subject's better self.

The advantages of well-designed custom-made wearables over off-the-peg are significant and self-evident. With proper rotation and care, handmade apparel will outlast any item produced in a factory. A custom-made suit will yield at least ten years of good service, while a handcrafted shoe can easily last over twenty years. Amortized over the life of the product, the cost per annum favors the custom-made quality.

However, value is not the primary reason many men prefer custom tailoring. In the bespoke world, everything revolves around the pampered customer—his build, posture, coloring, and personal taste dictate all. Buying custom clothes represents the sort of focused and efficient use of time that top executives try to cultivate throughout their business day. Additionally, the relationship forged over time between tailor and client can provide pleasure above and beyond the work produced by this alliance. Given the privacy and intimate attention afforded each customer by this process, a man can relax during his fitting and then return to the rigors of daily life refreshed.

Having described the real upside to the bespoke experience, we must now consider its potential downside. One of the inherent disadvantages of custom making is that the finished product cannot be judged until it is too far along to be substantially changed. Therefore, much depends on the taste and aesthetic sensibilities of the maker. If he adheres to the time-tested steps of the custom-tailoring tradition, the materials and workmanship that normally accompany such a process usually ensure the garment's superior quality. However, the quality of its design is another matter.

The highest-caliber workmanship or carriage-trade service will not undo the unsightliness of a poorly designed peaked lapel, an unflatteringly shaped dress shirt collar, or an inelegantly formed toe box. Whereas most men operating as custom makers are skilled craftsmen, their tastes tend to reflect their own working-class backgrounds. Many well-established firms are now owned by an employee who stepped out of the workroom to take over the business after the founder retired or passed on. Years of perfecting his craft hardly give him the appropriate social frame of reference to act as an arbiter of taste and style in this collaboration.

Examples of this can be found in most Hong Kong tailored clothes. Compared to the average ready-to-wear suit, the Hong Kong creation, which generally features better fabrics and workmanship, offers a good value. However, most are poorly designed, inexpensively finished, and, therefore, unsophisticated in appearance.

Choosing a custom maker is difficult for the man traveling in this rarefied world for the first time. Some protection is assumed if the choice is based on a friend's recommendation. However, you remove considerable risk from the selection process by employing an artisan who has a definable "house style." The finest bespoke firms are still thriving because their signature approach to design has transcended the vagaries of fashion as well as the tastes of their employees. Most of the top firms have their own long-considered ideas on what style shows off a man to his best advantage, and you should listen carefully to see if their beliefs reflect your own. Establishments that claim they will make "anything you want" are to be avoided, unless you yourself are a designer and are prepared to take responsibility for the garment's final form.

If you desire a look all your own, find a craftsman who already makes something recognizably close to what you want and is comfortable adapting it to your needs. I would not go to Bill Fioravanti in New York City for a soft-shouldered, drapey suit, just as I would not ask London's Anderson & Sheppard to make me a fitted, built-up, English-style hacking jacket. Such judgments are easier to reach, since these makers have a clear-cut point of view. While you cannot totally eliminate the risk factor from the custom-made product, choosing a craftsman with a "house look" minimizes the margin of surprise. However, in the hands of a craftsman with a strong sense of style, the outcome's unpredictability becomes part of the experience's attraction.

Equally important is understanding just how custom-made the article actually is. Today, the term "custom-made" has come to represent a wide range of different manufacturing processes and qualities, so caveat emptor. Legitimately bespoke products involve a specific series of steps with commensurate degrees of quality and thus price. If a customer is going to order something represented as custom-made, and he is going to receive something made by a different process, he should know this beforehand.

CUSTOM TAILORING

With retailers cutting back their slower-turning stocks of tailored clothing to bolster their cash flow, more stores than ever before are offering made-to-order clothes. And given the reduced selections and available sizes, more men are testing these waters. Because the price of a better designer or European hand-tailored, off-the-peg suit has, in some instances, surpassed that of one custom-made, the interest in bespoke clothing has increased. However, the first thing you must establish is to what degree the clothing you are about to order is genuinely custom-made.

The term "custom-made," when referring to tailored clothing, is used so loosely today—particularly by those who have something to gain by its obfuscation—that it is now applied to almost any garment that has not been purchased off the rack. However, the criteria for judging whether a man's tailored garment is authentically custom-made have changed little since the early part of the twentieth century. Four procedures must be observed if the product is to earn such a designation.

First, the individual parts must be cut from a paper pattern that has been created specifically for the wearer. In the old days, the tailor who measured the suit would cut the pattern immediately upon the client's departure. This meant the wearer's unique carriage and manner, elements that inform the garment's character, were kept fresh in his mind's eye. Second, the terminology presupposes that the material is of the highest caliber, the sewing thread of silk, the linings of fine silk or rayon bemberg, and the buttons of genuine horn or a vegetable derivative. Third, all the work required to create the suit was to be executed on the premises where the measurements were taken. This ensured authenticity and aesthetic consistency, and acted as a quality control. Finally, except for the straight seams of the trouser, all work was to be executed completely by hand.

The entire process required at least two or three fittings to take the garment from its first to final stage. The long-term advantage of having a suit made in this manner revolves around its original paper template. Once created, it can be adjusted to further perfect the next garment. Nothing controls the consistency of each subsequent suit's fit and look more precisely than this finite individual pattern.

One rung down from the custom-made, yet one rung above the ready-made, is the made-to-measure product. Made-to-measure defines a process rather than a specific level of craft, so these products can vary widely in quality and price. The made-to-measure garment can be tailored from a superior cloth or an inferior one, by hand or by machine.

Instead of a paper pattern being made expressly for the client, the manufacturer's stock pattern becomes the starting point. Various adjustments for fit are incorporated into it to individualize the final garment. The coat is delivered to the store without buttonholes, allowing the shop's fitter to position them correctly while the customer is wearing it. This technique for capturing a person's fit works well for most men, unless their posture or bone formation requires something more particular. How well it replicates the custom-made suit's fit depends upon the measuring tailor's expertise and the extent to which the base pattern can be manipulated to resemble an original pattern.

Today, a computer generates individual cutting instructions and a customer's pattern is created and retained to record subsequent alterations. If the customer's body reasonably approximates the stock pattern, the computerized pattern will provide a fit approaching the tailor-created custom blueprint. However, if the customer requires significant adjustments, the computer-generated individual pattern will not measure up.

Most of the nuances that distinguish one top custom tailor's work from another are too esoteric to describe in mere words. Before engaging any tailor, you should ask to see a recent sample of his work, preferably something that is about to be collected by its owner. Unfortunately, inspecting the jacket's cut or fit when it is not being worn by the body it was designed for won't be of much benefit, unless you are a tailor or bring a learned eye to such matters. Though its fabric, modeling, and detailing reflect the patron's wishes and most of its tailoring craft is concealed beneath its linings or shell fabric, you can learn much by examining the buttonholes. The sensibility and execution of the buttonholes reflect the creator's training and taste in a way that can be illuminating.

Examine the lapel buttonhole first. As the detail closest to the wearer's face, it offers the most visible evidence of the tailor's artistry. It is the last element of needlework to go into the garment before its final pressing. If its color, size, or placement is off, it can undo the forty or so hours of painstaking work invested in your garment. As founders of the woolen tailoring world, Savile Row tailors established the standards for high-class buttonhole decorum many years ago. Depending on where he apprenticed, each tailor on the Row may favor a different silhouette or style, but each jacket's buttonholes are a consistent part of this legendary culture's pedigree.

Creating a proper buttonhole is a dying art usually performed by trained women with exceptional finger dexterity. The lapel buttonhole should be long enough (1 inch to 1⅛ inches) to comfortably accommodate a flower, though you may never choose to wear one. There should be a keeper for the flower stem on the lapel's underside. The buttonhole should be precisely angled on the same line as the slope of the lapel's notch. If the coat has a peaked lapel, it should line up on the same angle as the peaked portion. If a flower were placed in it, it would be framed by the lapel's outer edges.

The buttonholes on the lapels and sleeves should be hand-sewn so skillfully that their individual stitches become hard to discern. Although there are sewing machines that try to simulate the look of a handmade buttonhole, legitimately custom-made clothes require that they be hand-sewn. Many tailors choose a machine-made buttonhole because their own hand-sewn buttonholes end up looking ragged, as if a dog had gnawed on them. A handmade buttonhole is clean on the outside and rough on the underside. A machine-made hole is clean on both sides. When finished, the buttonhole should be supple to the touch.

Quite important is its color, which should disappear into the cloth. For example, a buttonhole on a black-and-white glen plaid suit should have an inconspicuous, medium gray tint. If I saw a color such as charcoal gray or even black, contrasting upon such a cloth, as is found in most middle-brow custom-tailored clothes, I would note the tailor's lack of taste.

The jacket sleeve's buttonholes should be aligned straight and close enough to one another so that the buttons appear to kiss. The distance from the edge of the jacket's cuff to the middle of the first button should not exceed 1⅛ inches. More than that, and they look as if they are floating on the sleeve and have abandoned their historical relationship to the cuff as its fastener.

THE SYMBOLS OF CUSTOM TAILORING: HANDMADE, FUNCTIONAL JACKET SLEEVE BUTTONHOLES.

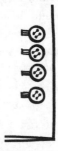

THE BUTTONHOLES' PLACEMENT INDICATES THE PEDIGREE OF THEIR TAILOR: THE BUTTON'S EDGES SHOULD KISS AND NOT REST TOO HIGH UP THE SLEEVE AS IN READY-TO-WEAR GARMENTS.

If a tailor seems knowing about buttonholes, I would defer to his judgment in other matters. This is critical, since no matter how specifically you instruct any tailor, many aesthetic judgments concerning taste are going to be made by him in the course of his work with little input from you, and these are the ones that will ultimately infuse the clothing with a sense of class and character.

CUSTOM SHIRTING

Besides the individualization of its styling, the advantages of the custom-made dress shirt over one that is ready-to-wear can be found in its precise fit as well as the superior

quality and taste of its fabrics. The most visible and important component of the dress shirt is its collar (see pages
31–34), and the bespoke process allows for one that is designed to best present the wearer's face. The fit of the dress
shirt's cuff to the wearer's hand, its second most noticeable
detail, is another area where the custom route is decidedly
the higher of the two roads.

In choosing a shirtmaker, you must inquire about
what process he will use to produce your shirt. The maker
should begin by creating an individual pattern from which
he makes a sample shirt. Having been worn and washed
several times at home, the shirt should be examined on your
body for final approval or further altering. After those washings, the collar should fit comfortably while still allowing for
some shrinkage. The shirtsleeve should still be long enough
to show $1/2$ inch of cuff from under the jacket sleeve and also
have enough length to offset further shrinkage.

If cut from a stock pattern rather than an individual
pattern, the shirt is not custom-made. In some cases, if you
are a standard fit, the shirt might require little adjustment,
but it would be inaccurate to call it bespoke. Shirts qualify-
ing as genuinely custom-made start at around $275, although
$400 is probably closer to the average price. One quick way
to determine such a provenance is if the shirt's cloth is 36
inches in width. This is easy enough to determine. Ask the
salesman to show you a bolt of the fabric and ask him to
measure its width. Until a few years ago, the most expensive
shirt fabrics were still woven on the slower, older Italian
or Swiss looms, which fabricated a more tightly constructed, luxurious hand than the newer, faster, 60-inch-
width-producing power looms. Increasingly, the more
cost-effective wider-width fabrics are replacing the narrower-
width cloths, so this criterion is not as definitive as it used to
be. However, for the moment, Italy and Switzerland are the

only countries producing this quality of shirtings, so if your shirt fabric cannot be traced to either of these countries, it's likely not top of the line.

To confirm a shirt's pedigree, you must establish the shirt's level of sewing artistry and manufacturing skill. The entire shirt, including its side seams, should be sewn with a single needle. This construction allows for the smallest stitches, the narrowest seams, and the most meticulous finishing. The shirt's side seams should be precisely narrow and the individual stitches on its collar so small as to be almost invisible. The collar and cuff linings should be cotton (not fused) and from Europe. Switzerland makes the best. The yoke on the back of a custom shirt should be made of two separate pieces joined in the center and the buttons should be genuine mother-of-pearl and attached by hand. If there is a monogram, it too should be hand-embroidered as opposed to machine-made.

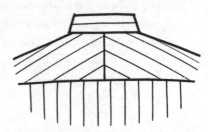

A TWO-PIECE (SPLIT) YOKE INDICATES THE POSSIBILITY THAT ONE SHOULDER IS HIGHER THAN THE OTHER AND HAS BEEN ACCOUNTED FOR IN THE SHIRT'S INDIVIDUAL DESIGN.

If the answers to these areas of investigation are satisfactory, you should be prepared to pay upward of $300 to $600, depending on the level of hand craftsmanship and fabric quality. Some makers include monograms or extra cuffs and collars. Choose to have the shirt's excess fabric set aside rather than made into a finished collar. If you lose or put on weight, it's better to have the fabric on hand. The costs can also vary according to the quality of two-ply cotton fabric used, which can range from 100s up to the very expensive, silklike 220s.

Of course, all things being equal, the ultimate value of

a bespoke dress shirt rests on the design and fit of its collar and cuffs as well as the nuances of its overall fit. However, there are some aspects of shirtmaking that do separate the masters from the top makers. These details include special gussets to reinforce the shirt's side seams where they meet at the hem bottom, pattern matching on the back yoke to the sleeve, hand-sewn buttonholes (found only in Europe), horizontal sleeve placket buttonholes, and extra-thick mother-of-pearl buttons (see pages 40–42).

All of the above qualify the product as custom-made. Below this, there are a variety of methods of individualized shirtmaking that are often called custom-made. Obviously, this term stands for a specific process of creating a particular shirt with an attendant quality of shirting fabric and shirtmaking. Made-to-order, individually cut, and made-to-measure are all terms that indicate something less than custom-made, and that is why they need to be understood if one is to compare apples with apples. If you pay less than $150 for a dress shirt and it is represented as being comparable to the top-of-the-heap bespoke ones, something is amiss. That is not to say that a custom-made shirt will always look better than a less expensive garment. A well-designed ready-to-wear or made-to-measure shirt with the right collar can look more flattering and thus provide more value than an expensive bespoke one with an inappropriately designed collar. As with all wearing apparel, design, not quality, is the ultimate arbiter of stylish longevity.

CUSTOM-MADE SHOES

The custom-made shoe represents the best return on investment of any article of male *habillement*. If you can afford the initial outlay of now $3,000 or more, you can amortize their cost over a ten- to thirty-year period. My own first pair of monogrammed velvet slippers is still going strong after twenty years of wear inside and outside the house.

Cobblers are distinguished from one another by their design sensibility. Any argument over the merits of a particular maker is usually a debate about taste rather than quality. The process of custom shoemaking is so particular and time-consuming that the handful of old-line firms still practicing the art do it pretty much as their forebears taught them. Once you have established that the creation procedure begins with your own carved wooden last, the tradition of bespoke footwear virtually guarantees the proven, time-honored sequence of handcrafting operations that will follow.

This means, to quote again the British cobbler John Lobb, "the last comes first." As a true representation of the client's foot, bunions and all, sculpted in wood, the last is everything in custom shoemaking. It determines the precise shape of the shoe that will eventually fit it. As long as the individual or firm crafting your shoe is prepared to invest the ten to twenty hours needed to properly sculpt this wooden form, the product's pedigree is assured. Some European cobblers make a temporary shoe to test out the last before going to a finished shoe. This is even more exacting and time-consuming and increases the expense and the odds of receiving a perfect fit—but the most important ingredient is still the artistry of the last.

Custom-made shoes enjoy three advantages over ready-to-wear—fit, quality, and style. Factory-made shoes require the wearer's foot to fit the shoe, a hit-or-miss proposition given the nuances of the individual foot. Custom-made shoes are constructed around such idiosyncrasies as bunions, calcifications, unusual toe joints, bone spurs, and crooked toes. The arch of a handmade shoe can be fitted up under the foot's instep, bolstering the arch while supporting the body's weight. The real art of a good handmade shoe can be found in its lightness and springiness to the step. Its weight-lessness can be deceiving, since it is probably solid enough to outlast its owner.

No machine yet invented can construct a shoe as fine as one made and stitched by hand. The thread used to stitch the leather on custom-made shoes is hemp. In some operations, eight to twelve pieces of it are rolled and waxed into a single twine, producing a stronger thread than that used in factory-made products. Machine stitching is just punched in and will never hold as long as those made by hand and individually locked in.

Handmade shoes employ costlier, higher quality leathers than factory-made ones and, when polished, produce a richer, deeper luster. Over time, the surface of brown hand-made shoes will develop a patina, much like the wood of some fine antique. The individual leather pieces that constitute the custom shoe's design are also more carefully matched than in the ready-made.

As for style, rest a handmade shoe next to one made by machine, and the custom's bevelled waist and closer-cut welts will graphically underscore its neighbor's bootlike clunkiness. The sculpting of the bespoke shoe's waist can make even the most ungainly foot appear sleek and smart. No machine-made toe box can ever be as elegantly crafted as one individually built by hand.

The difference between handmade and machine-made shoes becomes obvious when you examine their respective back quarters and heels. On a custom-made shoe, the instep

THE INSIDE BACK QUARTER OF A
HANDMADE SHOE IS CUT HIGHER ON
THE FOOT THAN THE OUTSIDE BACK
QUARTER. THIS SUPPORTS THE
INSIDE OF THE FOOT WHILE MAKING
THE FOOT APPEAR LIGHTER AND
MORE ELEGANT TO THE EYE.

side is cut higher on the foot than its outside back quarter. On the ready-made, the two sides are the same height. Top-quality heels are built from layers of leather held together by brass pins and have rubber tips to prevent slippage in bad weather. They are made to taper just so, while most ready-made heels resemble solid blocks. The curved pitch of the handmade shoe's back, when compared to the machine-made's regulation ninety-degree angle, conveys a graceful-ness seen only in cobbled footwear.

But perhaps the most significant distinction between individual and factory-produced shodding is the manner in which the custom-made shoe's shape follows the foot's natu-ral line. Much like the foot, the inside and outside lines of the handmade shoe have contrasting symmetries. The hand-made's outside line is curved, while the inside line is straight. The machine-made shoe, whose inside and outside lines almost approximate each other, looks as if it could have been stamped out with a cookie cutter, which, in many ways, is exactly how it has been produced (see page 126).

While each handcrafted-shoe firm has its own house

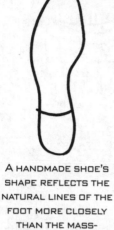

A HANDMADE SHOE'S
SHAPE REFLECTS THE
NATURAL LINES OF THE
FOOT MORE CLOSELY
THAN THE MASS-
PRODUCED SHOE.

A MACHINE-MADE
SHOE'S SHAPE
REQUIRES THE FOOT
TO CONFORM TO IT.

shape, it is the client's foot that will ultimately determine the product's final silhouette. However, no matter what shoe style the patron desires, these masters can design any model that will delight the foot as much as it will capture the eye.

Traveling with Your Wardrobe: Packing and Care

THE SECRETS OF WRINKLE-FREE TRAVEL

The basic objective of packing a suitcase is to get as much in as small a space as possible, while managing to arrive at your destination relatively wrinkle-free. An underpacked suitcase leaves too much room for clothes to shift and crunch. Conversely, an overpacked one produces hard-to-remove creases. When carefully folded and arranged, the contents of a suitcase should snugly fill its interior with its weight distributed equally throughout the bag for easier carrying.

Before making any other packing decisions, you must first choose the sort of luggage, hard or soft, that best fits your traveling requirements. While a hard suitcase offers your clothes greater protection and can be a terrific makeshift seat if there is nothing else available, its inflexibility can be a hindrance if you are forced to squeeze it into a tight, awkward storage area. Luggage made along the lines of the old-world-elegant Vuitton or Asprey's steamer trunks look exceptionally stylish, but they will also soon look exceptionally battered after being pummelled about in today's taxi trunks or airport conveyances. Of course, if you travel by limousine to a private jet or *Queen Elizabeth II*, such problems will be of little concern. But for those whose mode of transportation to the airport, dock, or train depot usually has a meter in the front seat, the luggage's vulnerability is an issue.

Softer cases give you greater flexibility around their sides; should you acquire anything during your travels, they can accommodate the additions more easily than harder luggage. They are also more manageable in difficult-to-fit spaces, a fact you'll appreciate if one ends up jammed beneath your legs. The softer bags range from the ballistic nylon—lightweight, slashproof, and Prada chic if well-designed and black—to the printed canvas and leather-trimmed bags by Vuitton, Gucci, and Etro, which last a lot longer than their soft appearance might suggest.

If you opt for the semistructured luggage, you should consider whether you will travel with a suitcase large enough to accommodate a single-folded coat or a garment bag. The idea that your clothing, especially your suits, should hang in your luggage just as they hang in your closet has made the garment bag a popular choice for many travelers.

Since packing and unpacking the garment bag are easy matters, overpacking the garment bag is always a temptation. So, when faced with a choice between the three- or four-suiter, give serious thought to the smaller of the two. Garment bags come with several zippered compartments, designed to hold specific items such as shoes or toiletries. The better ones come with a "wet" bag for damp exercise clothes or laundry and have compartments that are accessible from the inside as well as the outside. Choose one with mesh or clear vinyl compartments, so you can see whatever you are looking for without having to completely unpack. Also, be sure to find a bag that can utilize different types of hangers, so that you are not stuck if you lose or damage one. Garment bags can be heavy and unwieldy, so make sure yours has a wide, padded shoulder strap. Finally, whether you choose the suitcase or the garment bag, there is a technique to packing both.

PACKING

PACKING THE SUITCASE

As a first order of business, you must decide which articles will be packed at the bottom of your bag. Many experts recommend putting trousers in first, leaving the legs out until everything else is in, and then folding them over the top of the pile. I disagree with this on two counts. First, since the trouser would rest against the top and bottom sides of the suitcase, you risk exposing it to any number of hazards, including moisture, that could ruin not only the trouser but effectively the entire suit. Second, travelers often arrive at their destination without enough time to fully unpack before having to keep some business appointment or social engagement. Therefore, the last thing to pack is a suit, since it is the first item that you will want to hang up to air out and dewrinkle. The first thing you pack will have to absorb the full weight of the clothes placed on top of it. So the garment to place at the bottom of your bag should be some item like a sweater, jogging clothes, jeans, or bulky trousers, anything that can wrinkle or get wet without causing you anxiety.

While packing, place tissue paper or plastic between each layer of clothing. Acid-free, crinkly tissue paper is the butler-approved device, while plastic, which allows your clothes to slide rather than settle and crease, is a close second. As you pack these items, a small moat should form around your island of clothing. This is the place for your footwear. Since packing and unpacking exposes fine leather shoes to scratching, your shoes should be protected by bags. The best shoe bags are made of brushed felt, which shields the shoe's uppers while maintaining their polish. They also prevent the shoes from leaving polish marks on your suitcase or clothes. Plastic bags will not prevent scratches and scuffs and, if the climate is humid, can stick to the shoe, diminishing its luster. Face the soles of the bagged shoes against the walls of the case so that they are provided with the maximum protection while lending structure to the other packed garments.

Besides being covered, your shoes should be treed. Without travel shoe trees, your footwear may become deformed. Wooden trees are preferable, since they absorb moisture; shoe repair shops sell light plastic ones that will do in a pinch but should otherwise be avoided. If trees, plastic or otherwise, are unavailable, you can provide your shoes with temporary support by stuffing them with socks or underwear. Never separate a pair of shoes; if you pack a left and a right in different containers, you double the chances that the pair will not arrive intact. Once the shoes are positioned, soft items such as linen, hosiery, and handkerchiefs should be stuffed in the spaces between them to provide additional cushioning.

Dress shirts can now be added with their collars alternating at each end. A professionally folded dress shirt with collar support in the cleaner's plastic bag is going to emerge from its casing more wearable than the ones you folded yourself. Shirts folded off hangers always need more touching up than shirts folded by the cleaner. However, if you insist on folding them yourself, choose the "long" fold, with the shirt folded below the waistline, ensuring a crease-free belly. Rolled-up socks or underwear can be stuffed within the collar for additional support.

Everything that is now in your case should be firmly set in place. If the moat between the outside wall and your clothing island is well fortified, the contents should move as a unit while the surrounding items can move independently as the weight of the parcel is redistributed during travel. Your trousers, folded in two with each waistband alternating with the other, should be packed next. In between each trouser, place four or five neckties folded once in half. The trousers will keep them flat and any resulting crease in the tie will come at the back of the neck, where it is concealed by your collar. A traveling tie case offers an even safer mode of travel for your neckwear, and it can easily be hung in your closet.

THE SUIT COAT SHOULD BE FOLDED IN HALF, INSIDE OUT, TAKING CARE TO PUSH THE SHOULDERS THROUGH AS SHOWN.

Your jacket is the next article to go in. Experienced travelers pack the night before, leaving their tailored clothing out until the very last moment to save unnecessary creasing. Fold your jacket lengthwise in

THE SECOND FOLD OF THE JACKET SHOULD BE BETWEEN WAIST BUTTON AND TOP OF INSIDE POCKET—WRINKLES SHOW LESS HERE AND HANG OUT MORE EASILY.

half, inside out, taking care to push the shoulders through while making sure the sleeves meet each other inside and hang down without wrinkling. Place plastic inside the coat's vertical fold. If your case is not long enough to accommodate single folding, put a layer of plastic or tissue over the folded jacket and fold it a second time between the button nearest the waistline and the top of the inside pocket. This is one place where a recalcitrant fold will easily come out.

One of the final items for packing is the leakproof dopp kit, which allows for any last-minute additions. This can be used to plug up any gaps on the perimeter created by the stacking of the trousers and jackets. Just as with your first layer, the last thing to be placed over your suit jacket should be a robe, second coat, or even some plastic, anything that will prevent moisture from reaching the garments below.

Packing the Garment Bag

Experienced travelers who favor garment bags use their compartmentalized arrangement to their advantage. They lay out each outfit beforehand with a dress shirt placed under each jacket and several ties hung on top of the slacks. Tissue is placed in the jacket sleeves and between the jacket and trouser. Each ensemble is encased by a plastic dry cleaning bag before it is hung in the garment bag. Folded dress shirts are never left at the bag's bottom where they can be crushed if a hanger falls.

PERMANENT PACKING FOR
FREQUENT TRAVELERS

Accoutrements

1. Small travel jewelry box for spare cuff links, collar bar pin, collar stays
2. Extra shoelaces in black or brown
3. Sewing kit with two different-sized needles; black, beige, and white thread; and several extra shirt buttons

4. Safety pins, small Swiss Army knife, and tape in case a cuff comes undone and emergency surgery is required
5. Travel alarm clock to back up the hotel wake-up call
6. Extra pair of reading glasses
7. Suede brush and whisk brush
8. Six to twelve plastic shirt bags to aid your packing

A word of warning: if you include any bottles in your bag, make sure they are unbreakable. Never place a breakable bottle in your bag unless it is packed in a leakproof container.

CARE FOR THE TRAVELER'S WARDROBE

TAILORED CLOTHING

As soon as you reach your destination, unpack and hang up your tailored clothes. Jackets should always be hung on wooden, wishbone-style hangers. Wire hangers are the bane of good clothes, so avoid hanging your jackets from them. Ordinary wooden hangers are an acceptable alternative if the heavier wishbone hangers are unavailable. The trousers can be folded over the center bar. However, it is always better to suspend them by their cuffs from a clip hanger, or, if your hotel is really classy and provides them, small wood trouser hangers with felt pads to prevent the trouser cuffs from wrinkling. When suspended by the cuffs, the full weight of the trouser is brought to bear, retaining the unbroken crease down the leg. If there is no time to have your clothes professionally pressed, hanging a suit in a steamy bathroom and then letting it dry in a cool room is a good way to remove its wrinkles. A good-quality travel press can also work the wrinkles out.

Try to arrange your schedule so your clothes can be properly pressed after unpacking. A freshly pressed suit will always look better than one that was pressed just prior to packing. If you have your suit pressed at the hotel, find out what quality of work it provides. Too often, either dry cleaning chemicals or an inexperienced presser can take the life and bounce out of a fine suit. Fine tailors prefer to do their own pressing when possible, because a bad press can ruin a well-made suit, while a good one can totally rejuvenate one. Ask the hotel's concierge or valet service to have your garments soft-pressed by hand. Tell them you want the jacket's lapels soft-rolled and the trousers steamed, brushed, and hand finished.

Avoid dry-cleaning a suit unless it is absolutely necessary, for instance if perspiration has seeped completely through it. Other than a light-colored summer suit, if the suit becomes stained, have it spot-cleaned first, then pressed. It is important to attach a note to the garment, telling the cleaner what caused the blemish. Technology has developed specific chemicals to combat specific stains. If the spot were red and the cleaner suspected raspberries were the culprit, he might try a fruit cleaning agent, whereas if it were blood, a protein-based solvent would be in order. Allow the cleaner as much time as he needs to deal with the stain. Some stains never get properly removed because the job was rushed to meet the traveler's schedule.

If you spill something, blot it up immediately. The more you get out of the fabric, the less there will be to eradicate later. Putting seltzer or water on oil-based stains such as salad dressing, mayonnaise, and the like only spreads the surface of the stain, making it ten times harder to remove. For water-soluble spills such as wine, the soiled garment should be placed on top of a dry, flat surface where it can be daubed with a warm, wet cloth. If it needs further attention, the spot can be dispatched with proper dry cleaning. Some food stains are harder to remove than others, therefore the more time you allow the cleaner, the better the chance of receiving a spotless garment.

DRESS SHIRT CARE

Nothing discourages a man from investing in an expensive dress shirt more than the prospect of having it professionally cleaned. Few places know how to press one properly. However, armed with some specific instructions, you can contain the damage and even be pleasantly surprised by the results. First, do not dry-clean dress shirts. Cotton dress shirts surrender their fresh, linenlike crispness and eventually turn gray if regularly dry-cleaned. Some men mistakenly believe this is the only way to prevent the garment from shrinking. Far better to buy a shirt in a size that allows for shrinkage.

Never allow a partially soiled dress shirt to be pressed; the heat from the iron can permanently "cook" the dirt into the fabric. Ask the laundry to wash the shirt separately without machine drying. Most shirts are washed en masse, which just spreads the dirt from one garment to another. Request that the shirt be hand-pressed—never allow it to be machine pressed—with as little starch in the collar and cuffs as you can bear. Heavy starch reduces the life of the collars and cuffs and accelerates their shrinkage.

SHOE CARE

The only thing profligate about owning expensive shoes is scrimping on their care. Plastic shoe trees do to shoes what wire hangers do to jackets—avoid them if at all possible.

Wooden shoe trees are the best protection your investment can have and should be inserted as soon as the shoe is removed from the foot. The shoe's interior is subject to some astonishing conditions, including continual moisture, heat, friction, and bacterial growth. Its exterior is exposed to heat, cold, precipitation, chemicals, abrasions, and good old-fashioned grime. Shoes must be rotated and allowed time to dry out. Wooden trees speed the drying process, deodorize, and prevent wet shoes from curling at the toe. If the shoes have been soaked, keep them away from heat, which can crack the leather. Stuffing them with newspaper will draw the moisture from the leather. Once they have dried, buff them with a soft cloth.

Leather is a skin, so treat it with the same care as you would your own. Shoes must be polished for protection and appearance. The first step I would take with a new pair of shoes is to treat them to the best shine available. There is nothing worse than getting a scuff mark on some unprotected portion of a new shoe; it will be with you in some form for the remainder of the shoe's life. Wax, which shields the leather against the elements, should be the first layer applied to the shoe. Polish is used only to achieve surface luster and should not be used as a substitute. Do not take your shoes out into the rain without first making sure they are protected by a good coat of polish. You should also polish the stitches of the shoe's welts; this helps to waterproof them.

CARING FOR YOUR NECKTIES

No stain is more difficult to remove than the one that lands on your silk necktie. However, if cleaned properly, most stains can be removed, provided the soiled tie has not sat for months in the back of your closet. This task should be performed by a professional service, such as New York City's Tiecrafters, Inc. (www.tiecrafters.com), which has the special equipment to press and roll the tie back into its original shape. Avoid cleaners who claim they can do this, because most will not invest money in such expensive machinery for the few neckties they clean each month.

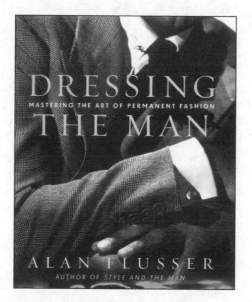

Dressing the Man is the definitive guide to what men need to know in order to dress well and look stylish without becoming fashion victims.

Alan Flusser's name is synonymous with taste and style. With his new book, he combines his encyclopedic knowledge of men's clothes with his signature wit and elegance to address the fundamental paradox of modern men's fashion: Why, after men today have spent more money on clothes than in any other period of history, are there fewer well-dressed men than at any time ever before?

According to Flusser, dressing well is not all that

difficult; the real challenge lies in being able to acquire the right personalized instruction. Dressing well pivots on two pillars—proportion and color. Flusser believes that "Permanent Fashionability," both his promise and goal for the reader, starts by being accountable to a personal set of physical trademarks and not to any kind of random, seasonally served-up collection of fashion flashes.

Unlike fashion, which is obliged to change each season, the face's shape, the neck's height, the shoulder's width, the arm's length, the torso's structure, and the foot's size remain fairly constant over time. Once a man learns how to adapt the fundamentals of permanent fashion to his physique and complexion, he's halfway home.

Taking the reader through each major clothing classification step-by-step, this user-friendly guide helps you apply your own specifics to a series of dressing options, from business casual and formal wear to pattern-on-pattern coordination, or how to choose the most flattering clothing silhouette for your body type and shirt collar for your face.

A man's physical traits represent his individual road map, and the quickest route toward an enduring style of dress is through exposure to the legendary practitioners of this rare masculine art. Flusser has assembled the largest and most diverse collection of stylishly mantled men ever found in one book. Many never-before-seen vintage photographs from the era of Cary Grant, Tyrone Power, and Fred Astaire are employed to help illustrate the range and diversity of authentic men's fashion. *Dressing the Man*'s sheer magnitude of options will enable the reader to expand both the grammar and the verbiage of his permanent fashion vocabulary.

For those men hoping to find sartorial fulfillment somewhere down the road, tethering their journey to the mind-set of permanent fashion will deliver them there earlier rather than later in life.